Rudolf Höfling

MiG
Aircraft Since 1939

MiG

Aircraft Since 1939

Rudolf Höfling

Pen & Sword
AVIATION

First published in Great Britain in 2015 by
Pen & Sword Aviation
an imprint of
Pen & Sword Books Ltd
47 Church Street
Barnsley
South Yorkshire
S70 2AS

ISBN 978 1 78383 170 8

A CIP catalogue record for this book is available from the British Library

Typeset in Ehrhardt by
Mac Style Ltd, Bridlington, East Yorkshire
Printed and bound in Malta by Gutenberg Press

Pen & Sword Books Ltd incorporates the imprints of Pen & Sword
Archaeology, Atlas, Aviation, Battleground, Discovery, Family History, History,
Maritime, Military, Naval, Politics, Railways, Select, Transport, True Crime,
and Fiction, Frontline Books, Leo Cooper, Praetorian Press, Seaforth
Publishing and Wharncliffe.

For a complete list of Pen & Sword titles please contact
PEN & SWORD BOOKS LIMITED
47 Church Street, Barnsley, South Yorkshire, S70 2AS, England
E-mail: enquiries@pen-and-sword.co.uk
Website: www.pen-and-sword.co.uk

My thanks go to the following persons who made available photographs for
this book: Ing.Karl Brandel, Hans-Jürgen Becker, Dipl.Ing.Jerzy Butkiewicz,
Peter P.K.Herrendorf, Guido Hitzenhammer, Laszlo Javor, Georg Mader,
Thomas Lakatha and Erich Strobl.

Contents

The History of the Firm at a Glance

In contrast to other well known aircraft manufacturers, OKB (Osboye Konstuktorskoye Bureau) Mikoyan-Gurevitch confined itself, with a few exceptions, to the design and construction of fighter aircraft. The first MiG aircraft appeared shortly before the entry of the USSR into the Second World War and until the arrival of the MiG 15, the second jet-fighter main type, the propellor-driven products of the manufacturer played a low-key role on the fighting front. At the end of the 1940s the comet-like rise of Mikoyan-Gurevitch began, until finally the name became the best known aircraft producer worldwide.

Anushavan "Artem" Ivanovitch Mikoyan was born on 5 August 1905 as the youngest of five children of a carpenter in the small mountain village of Sanain (today Tumanyan) in Armenia, near the Turkish border. Although the circumstances of his family were very modest, his mother insisted on a good education for her children. For this reason at age 13 Anushavan was sent to live with relatives at Tiblisi where he not only received a better education but also came into contact with Bolshevik politics. He had been fascinated by aircraft since seeing an emergency-landed Farman biplane as a child, and wanted to be a pilot. Lack of funds and tuberculosis, from which he never completely recovered, brought his education to an abrupt end. After secondary school he obtained work a a toolmaker at Rostov and subsequently at the Dynamo factory in Moscow until conscripted int the Red Army in 1925 in which he was then du bound to join the Communist party of the Sovie Union.

After one year's army service his talent and active work for the Communist Party gave Mikoyan the chance to become a student at th Shukovski Air Force Academy at Frunse where

For their graduation piece at the Shukovski Air Force Academy, Artem Mikoyan and other students built the light aircraft "Oktyabryonok".

Aircraft type:	Oktyabryonok
Purpose:	Trainer and sports aircraft
Crew:	One, no passengers
Drive:	1 two-cylinder P.Labur 25 hp engine
Wingspan:	8 m, length 6.2 m, height 2.76 m
Wing area:	11.4 sq.m
Weight empty:	150 kgs
Take-off weight:	264 kgs
Fuel and lubricant:	20 kgs
Ceiling:	3,000 m
Top speed:	126 kms/hr

Artem I. Mikoyan (centre) and Michail J Gurevitch (right).

1936/37 together with K. Samarin and N. A. Pavlov he worked on the construction of a light aircraft "Oktyabryonok" designed by Pjetr D. Grushin for his diploma. He graduated the following year. The testing of this high-wing monoplane with open cockpit began in November 1937 and was subsequently recommended for series production as a training aircraft or DIY version for aerial sporting clubs. "Oktjabryonok" (October child) meant six to ten year old children in the Communist pioneer organisations.

In the summer of 1937 Mikoyan was recruited by the newly established OKB (Experimental Construction Bureau) of Nikolai Nikolayevitch Polikarpov and joined the group working on the development of the Polikarpov I-153 fighter.

The other half of the future OKB MiG, Michail Josifovitch Gurevitch, was born on 12 January 1893 near Kursk, the son of a family of academics. He studied initially at the University of Kharkov, then at the Aeronautical Academy in Paris and finally at Kharkov again, at the Technical Institute, from where he graduated in 1923. Subsequently he joined CCB and in 1928

worked on engine design at the technical office of Frenchman Paul Aimé Richard who began work that same year in Moscow on his torpedo-carrying aircraft project TOM-1 for the Soviet naval air force. At the conclusion of this work in 1931, Gurevitch went over to Sergei A. Kotcherigin to head the TSh-3 project, an armoured attack aircraft. One of his most important colleagues there was Sergei W. Ilyushin who about ten years later would become famed even in the West for his Il-2 armoured fighter bomber and the coining of the term "Shturmovik". In 1936 Gurevitch accompanied his new director, Boris Lisunov, to the Douglas Aircraft Company at Santa Monica in the United States where both worked until early 1939 familiarising themselves with the technical side of the production of the Douglas DC-3 under licence – copied in the Soviet Union as the Lisunov Li-2.

After returning home, and while Lisunov began work in 1940 on the production of the DC-3 under licence, Gurevitch went over to the

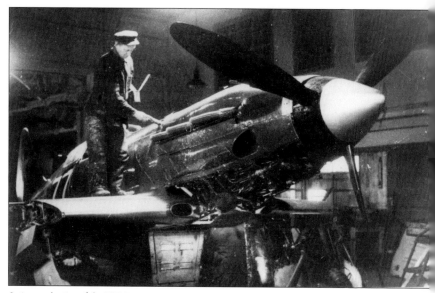

Series production of the MiG-3.

Polikarpov design office where he met Mikoyan for the first time. It was soon apparent that the two engineers, who also had a good private relationship, were an outstanding work team and they were soon given their own development group.

In July 1938, Polikarpov had begun his project K(WP) for a high-altitude aircraft designated I-61, and the following year passed the continuation of the work to the officially independent OKO-1 (Experimental Development Division) to be headed by Mikoyan. It was here that Mikoyan and Gurevitch worked for the first time together with other designers on a joint project. OKO-1 was established officially under Mikoyan's direction on 25 December 1939, occupying the GAZ-1 (National Aircraft Factory) "Osoaviachim" building in Moscow. This development was favoured by the influence of Mikoyan's elder

brother, Anastas Mikoyan, a member of the Politbureau and People's Commissar for Overseas Trade. A short while later OKO-1 became an independent design office as a result of Nikolai Polikarpov falling into disfavour in the Soviet Union at the highest level – a fate he shared with other Russian aircraft designers.

In October 1941 the entire concern was evacuated to Kuybishev in Siberia before the advance of the German Wehrmacht. Once the danger of invasion for the Soviet capital had been beaten off, on 16 March 1942 OKO-1 returned to Moscow to re-establish itself at the National Aircraft Factory (GAZ)-155 in Ulansky Alley. From this month the development bureau was also designated OKB 155 (MiG) and OKO MiG. The first development from this office was the MiG-1, quickly succeeded by the MiG-3 after a series of flaws came to light.

Although the fighting forces had only limited enthusiasm for this second muster, it remained at the front for the rest of the war. The subsequent fighter designs to appear during the Second World War were either prototypes or research machines. A major handicap of all these projects was frequently imperfect engine development. The great success for OKB 155 (MiG) came only at the end of the 1940s with its jet aircraft. Coincidentally the word "mig" in Russian colloquial speech means "moment", "in a flash", "in a trice" and is therefore used to indicate tempo and speed – which corresponds very appropriately to most of the aircraft projects of OKO MiG. The two engineers once specified that speed and altitude were from the outset to be dominant in the development philosophy of their aircraft. Therefore it was also only logical that the OKB 155 (MiG) from the beginning of 1944 would work on an appraisal of two captured Luftwaffe Me 163B rocket fighters with a view to copying the design but fitted with a Russian propulsion system.

With the exception of the work on the experimental jet engine RD-1 of the designers Lyulka, Dushkin and Glushkov begun in 1937, suspended when the Third Reich attacked the Soviet Union in June 1941, and the VRD-2, on which Lyulka worked in 1943 – but which was too weak as the propulsion for a fighter – there was no comparable research in the Soviet Union. The interest of the Soviet leadership in jet engines received a boost when in 1944/1945 the Red Army captured a number of German Junkers Jumo 004 and BMW 003 turbines. Research and copying began even before the war ended. The Jumo 004B became the further development RD-10 and the BMW 003A the RD-20, and both were turned out in series production. A few weeks before the war ended all development bureaux in the Soviet Union with experience in fighter production were given

The MiG-3 fighter at the GAZ-155 factory being handed over to the 12.IAP in the winter of 1942.

Detailed inspection of a MiG-15 (Georg Mader).

orders to develop jet fighters with at least top speed of 900 kms/hr. Thus Lavatshkin developed the La-150 and Yakovlev the Yak-15, both at OKB, both aircraft having an RD-10 jet engine. At OKB Suchoi the Su-9 appeared, clearly similar to the Messerschmitt Me 262 but powered by two RD-20 engines. (The designation Suchoi Su-9 was later changed to mean from the end of the 1950's a supersonic interceptor fighter, Air Standards Coordinating Committee code "Fishpot", a competitive prototype of the Mikoyan-Gurevitch MiG-21 "Fishbed".) The OKB 155 (MiG) submitted with its design I-300 a fighter aircraft with two RD-20 turbojets.

At the end of the Second World War numerous developments in jet aircraft by the victorious Powers were based on German research work and most Soviet aircraft designers from 1946 experienced problems in completing further development of German jet engines, surfaces and airframes for supersonic flight. Therefore Soviet Air Minister Michail Krunishev and aircraft designer Yakovlev suggested to Stalin that the British be requested to sell them some of their advanced developments, to which Stalin replied, "And what idiots would sell us their secrets?" Nevertheless Stalin gave the idea his support and accordingly Mikoyan, the engine builder Vladimir Klimov and other

representatives of the Soviet aeronautical industry travelled the same year to Great Britain to ask them for their latest jet designs. To the great astonishment of the Soviets the Labour Government of the time and its pro-Soviet Trade Minister Sir Stafford Cripps supported the Russians in their application to build the Rolls-Royce Nene-jet engine under licence. The first ten of these were sold to the Soviet Union the same autumn and designated RD-45. A further fifteen Nene-jet turbines followed in March 1947, and more later. By December 1948 this British jet engine had been developed into the Klimov VK-1 and went immediately into series production. A thousand VK-1's were manufactured, but the Rolls-Royce firm never recuperated a penny of its licence dues of 207 million pounds sterling from the Soviet Union.

By virtue of its turbojets OKB MiG began its unparalleled rise, for the VK-1 became the standard jet engine in various versions of the worldwide successes MiG-15 and MiG-17. These two jets were an unpleasant surprise for their enemies over Korea and Vietnam. Since the Second World War it had been thought in the West that Soviet technological advances lagged behind those of the West, although in many aspects this was true. An even greater surprise for the West was the appearance of the MiG-21 at the end of the 1950s. Just as the heads of the Soviet air force V-VS wanted a Dassault Mirage III for a closer look, so the Americans wanted a MiG-21. This led to the United States offering a bounty of US$125,000 for an undamaged "Fishbed", and prompted several MiG pilots to defect over the next few years.

In subsequent decades at OKB MiG, a series of different designers worked as senior engineers on a number of projects. On 20 December 1956 Mikoyan was appointed Senior

Designer. Eight years later Gurevitch was pensioned off on health grounds and Mikoyan remained until his retirement the sole head of the design bureau. On 27 May 1969 Colonel-General of the Technical Services Anushavan Mikoyan died of a heart attack and in the following year the firm was turned into the limited company A. I. Mikoyan so that while the name Gurevitch was dropped the abbreviation MiG was retained. In succeeding years this limited company became the most significant development centre for fighter aircraft in the Soviet Union, whose employees proudly referred to themselves as "Mikoyanovzi". The frequent supremacy of MiG aircraft over competitors in the Soviet Union was seen not only in their performance but also in the enormous numbers produced. Thus OKB MiG turned out besides 134 prototypes around thirty series-produced aircraft types. Furthermore the MiG-15 and MiG-17 were the most frequently built aircraft worldwide in the speed class to Mach 1 – the MiG-21, in service with 49 air forces, was the most frequently built aircraft worldwide in the Mach 2 class and even the MiG-25 has its place in air force history as the first Mach-3 aircraft to enter series production.

Because Mikoyan and Gurevitch developed so many aircraft types, only the most important of them are reviewed in this book, arranged in order from the maiden flight.

A detailed inspection of a Slovak MiG-21MF at the Malacky air force base, 1994.

A-144	2	I-307	1
ATTA 3000	2 with Promavia S.A.	I-308	1
E-2	3 of which two E-2A	I-310	3
E-4	2	I-312	1
E-5	2	I-320	3
E-6	3	I-330	1
E-7	2	I-340	1
E-8	2	I-350	1
E-9	1	I-360	1
E-23	1	I-370	1
E-26	1	K-1	1
E-33	2	MiG-AT	less than 100 (Western estimate)
E-50	3		
E-66	2	MiG-1	100
E-074	1	MiG-3	3,120
E-76	1	MiG-4	1 (mock-up)
E-77	1	MiG-5	2 DIS and DIS-T MiG-6 only project
E-88	1		
E-150	1	MiG-8 "Utka"	1
E-151	only a project	MiG-9	604
E-152	3	MiG-13	25
E-155	10	MiG-15	more than 18,000 (Western estimate)
E-166	1 (actually E-152-1)		
E-231	1	MiG-17	15–16,000 (Western etimate)
E-266	2 former E-155	MiG 19	about 8,500 (Western estimate)
I-2	1	MiG-21	about 12,000 (without China)
I-3	2	MiG-25	more than 1,500
I-5	1	MiG-23 "Faceplate"	5 pre-series of E-2A
I-7	1	MiG 23	more than 3,100 (Western estimate)
1-200	3		
I-210	5	MiG-27	see MiG-23
I-211	11 pre-series	MiG-29	more than 1,700 (Western estimate)
I-220	2		
I-221	1	MiG-31	more than 200 (Western estimate)
I-222	1		
I-224	1	MiG-33	only project
I-225	2	MiG-35	see MiG-29
I-230	5 pre-series	MiG-101	only project
I-231	1	MiG-110	1
I-250	2	MiG-105/11	1 or 3
I-270	2	MiG-121	at the time only a project
I-300	3	MiG 1.42+MiG 1.44	4 of which 2 airframes
I-301	3	"Oktyabryonok"	at least 1
I-302	1	SVB "Highlander"	only project
I-305	1	TA-4	1

MiG-1

In January 1939 NKAP (People's Commissariat for the Aviation Industry) laid down the specification for an all-purpose fighter similar to the Messerschmitt Bf 109. Ten Soviet development bureaux tendered ideas, including Yakovlev, Lavotshkin and Polikarpov. In July 1939 the OKO-1 in Moscow, a branch of OKB Polikarpov, began work under the leadership of Mikoyan on the prototype I-61 with project code K, which was more a high-altitude fighter than a general purpose aircraft. A 1380-hp V-12 motor Mikulin AM 37F with 1400 hp was planned, which would be a further development of the older AM-35 plant. Because a series of modifications were introduced to the prototype during the development, it was renumbered I-200 in January 1940. Technical problems with the new engine caused repeated

Aircraft type:	MiG-1
Purpose:	High altitude aircraft
Crew:	One
Engine plant:	1 Mikulin AM-35A V12 motor, 1350 hp
Wingspan:	10.2 m, length: 8.16 m, height: 2.62 m
Wing surface:	17.44 sq.m
Weight empty:	2630 kgs
Normal take-off weight:	3071 kgs
Top speeds:	(low-level) 508 kms/hr, (7000 m) 628 kms/hr (7200 m) 648 kms/hr
Ceiling:	12,000 m
Rate of climb to 5,000 m:	5 mins 18 secs
Range:	730 kms
Armament:	1 x 12.7 mm UBS MG with 300 rounds, 2 x 7.62mm SchKAS MG each with 375 rounds, up to 200 kgs bombload under the wings

The I-200, begun as I-61 in July 1939 at OKB Polikarpov, led in the summer of 1940 to the MiG-1, the first design of Mikoyan and Gurevitch.

A total of 100 MiG-1's were produced in series, the sliding hood was not installed until the ninth model.

delays in finishing the I-200 so that for the first trial flight a 1350 hp AM-35A motor was installed. On 5 April 1940 the prototype made its maiden flight and the second I-200 flew on 9 May 1940 – afterwards it was designated MiG-2 for two months – and the third I-200 flew for the first time on 6 June.

Though attaining a speed of 648.5 kms/hr on 24 May 1940, the manouvrability of the first prototype was not acceptable, for its permanent inclination to tail-spin was dangerous. There were also over-heating problems in the engine. Because the I-200 was too heavy, the armament had to be limited to 50 kgs, which meant smaller calibre MGs. Added to these drawbacks were deficiencies in manufacture which led to engine failure causing one prototype to crash.

As a result of the poor experience with the prototype I-200 the Soviet Air Force demanded an urgent revision of the high-altitude fighter concept while allowing the series production to proceed. Parallel to the batch of 100 series aircraft being turned out a programme of improvements was begun. In the summer of 1940 the prototype I-200 received the official designation MiG-1. In order to increase its range, the last machines of the run were given outboard tanks. The one-hundredth and last MiG-1 left State Aircraft Factory-1 (GAZ-1) on 5 December 1940 and the same day preparation for the successor in series MiG-3 was begun. The first MiG-1's were not delivered to the Soviet Air Force until the autumn of 1940.

■ **14**

MiG-3

At the end of 1940 the Soviet Air Force still had a pressing need for a reliable high-altitude machine after the MiG-1 had shown itself to be unripe. Therefore the type was subjected to more testing for its further development in the TsAG1 wind tunnel. The MiG-1 engine plant was retained for the MiG-3: the wingspan was the same but the fuselage 10 cms longer than the predecessor and heavier. Some MiG-3 reconnaissance aircraft had one or two cameras installed in the fuselage.

On 5 December 1940 the majority of the modifications to the new aircraft were completed and at GAZ-1 the first of the series followed the last of the MiG-1's the same day. In December of the following year Stalin awarded the highest priority to the ground attack aircraft Ilyushin Il-2 "Shturmovik" and in order to raise the production capacity of the

Aircraft type:	MiG-3
Purpose:	High-altitude fighter
Crew:	One
Engine plant:	1 Mikulin AM 35A V12-engine, 1350 hp
Wingspan:	10.2 m
Length:	8.25 m
Wingspan:	17.44 sq.m
Weight empty:	2699 kgs, max
Take-off weight:	3350 kgs
Top speeds:	(low level) 495 kms/hr at 7800 m, 495 kms/hr
Ceiling:	12,500 m
Rate of climb (5000 m):	5 mins 18 secs (8000 m) 10 mins 17 secs.
Range:	820 kms
Armament:	1 x 12.7 mm UBS MG, 300 rounds: 2 x 7.62mm SchKAG MG, 375 rounds each
Additional load:	up to 220 kgs bombload at four points below the wings

The MiG-3 resulted from permanent improvements during the series run of the MiG-1 (Georg Mader).

Mikulin AM-38-V engine for the Il-2 a halt was called to the work on the AM-35A engine.

The MiG-3 series run was terminated on 23 December 1941 with the 3,120th machine. In June 1941 the front line squadrons had 845 MiG-3s operational, almost 15% of all Soviet fighter aircraft. By 6 July 1941 a total of 79 MiG-3s, incorrectly assumed by the Germans to be I-18's, had fallen into Wehrmacht hands more or less damaged.

Between May and August 1941 a MiG-3 of the series production was tested in flight with an experimental 1400 hp Mikulin AM 37F V-12 engine and designated MiG-7 and MiG 3/AM-37. In August 1941 the AM-37F was exchanged for one of the new 1600 hp Mikulin AM-38 V12 engines and flight-tested. In the next few months after testing, this aircraft, now designated MiG-3/AM-38, had as expected a better performance than the series variant, but was not a high-altitude fighter. As the Mikulin AM-38 engines were required at this point for the Il-2 ground attack aircraft, this MiG variant did not enter series production although the eighty or so damaged MiG-3's which went to the works for repair were fitted with AM-38 engine plant there.

The serious lack of Mikulin engines for the MiG-3 led in October 1941 to the search for alternatives. Thus from August/September 1941 GAZ-1 works had installed experimentally in five MiG-3 mainframes 1700-hp Shvetzov M-82A 14-cylinder double-radial motors.

The mounting of the engine plant required a change in the cockpit, rear fuselage and an enlargement of the rudder gear. All this work to

The series production of the MiG-3 followed the 100th MiG-1 (Georg Mader).

This MiG-3 was demonstrated during the MAKS 2007 in Moscow. (Georg Mader)

A non-flyable replica of a MiG-3 exhibited at Monino.

find a new engine for the MiG-3 series production, under great pressure, was carried out more from experience than scientificallly. The MiG-3/M-82 prototypes were also known as MiG-9, Ikh and I-210. The maiden flight of a MiG-3/M-82 on 2 January 1942 provided a below-average flight performance, strong vibrations and other defects. The test phase of the I-210 was accordingly soon ended and the five prototypes were given more armament before being sent to the Kalinin Front and the project abandoned.

MiG-4

In May 1940 the Soviet Air Force authorised the development of an armoured ground attack aircraft at OKN-1 and designated the project PBSh-1 and MiG-4. The plan was for an armoured, single-seat monoplane with reverse gull-wing configuration and a wheeled chassis retractable to the middle of the fuselage. The 1,390 kgs of armour was a major contribution to the total weight allowance. The rounds from the VJ-23 MGs could penetrate armour over 25 mms thick at long range and were therefore expected to be effective against most known armour of the time. In addition the aircraft could carry up to twelve RS-82 rockets or combinations of bombloads. The bombs envisaged were either 24 FAB-10, 24 FAB-8, 28 FAB-2 or 120 ZAB-1. For dive-bomber attacks against the larger kind of armoured target the PBSh-1 could also carry two FAB-250 bombs. A full-scale mock-up of the MiG-4 was exhibited

Aircraft type:	MiG-4
Purpose:	Ground attack aircraft prototype
Crew:	One
Engine plant:	1 x Mikulin AM-38 V 12-engine, 1600 hp (planned)
Weight empty:	4850 kgs, max
Take-off weight:	6024 kgs
Top speed:	(low level) 449 kms/hr (estimated), at 7800 m, 640 kms/hr
Ceiling:	7,600 m (estimated)
Range:	900 kms (estimated)
Armament:	2 x 23mm VJ 23 MK with 96 rounds, 6 x 7.62mm SchKAS MG with 750 rounds each, bombload up to 500 kgs

to repesentatives of the Soviet Air Force on 24 July 1940, but the project was abandoned soon afterwards because a better performance was expected from its successor PBSh-2 (MiG-6).

The escort-fighter prototype MiG-5 (DIS) was fitted with Mikulin series engines.

MiG-5

Under the direction of Pietr D. Grushin, who joined OKO-1 in the summer of 1940, a development team was formed which began work in August 1940 on the twin-engined escort fighter DIS, a competitor to the Polikarpov TIS. Because the Ach diesels from A. D .Charmovski planned for this heavy fighter were not yet available, 1400 hp Mikulin AM-37 V12 engines were fitted instead. This aircraft, which took to the air for the first time on 15 May 1941, was designated Aircraft T internally at the works with the result that the first prototype received the name DIS-T. The performance in the air of this heavy fighter, known for a time as the MiG-2, was satisfactory. It was decided during the weeks of flight testing to equip the machine with two FAB-500 bombs to be released when diving. It was also considered producing a torpedo-bomber version of the DIS-T.

When in October 1941 OKO-1 was evacuated from Moscow to Kuybishev at the approach of the Wehrmacht, DIS-T transferred to Kazan. At Kuybishev a short while later the second prototype DIS-IT/DIS-200 was completed. This aircraft had an engine plant of two 14-cylinder Shvetzov M-82F radial engines and made its maiden flight on 22 January 1942. Later the DIS-200 joined its predecessor DIS-T at Kazan where both twin-engined aircraft remained until they were scrapped. Despite the promising performance of both fighters, there was a shortage of material over these months

Aircraft type:	MiG-5
Purpose:	Escort fighter-prototype (DIS), fighter-bomber (DIS-T)
Crew:	1
Engine plant (DIS):	2 x Mikulin AM-37 V12 engines each 1400 hp
Engine plant (DIS-T):	2 x Shvetzov M-82F 14-cylinder double radial engines, each 1400 hp
Wingspan:	15.1 m (DIS), length: 10.87 m (DIS), 12.14 m (DIS-T), wing surface, 38.9 sq.m (DIS)
Weight empty:	6140 kgs (DIS)
Take-off weight:	(DIS) 8060 kgs; (DIS-T) 8000 kgs
Top speed:	(5,000 m): 604 kms/hr (DIS-T) (6,800 m) 610 kms/hr (DIS)
Ceiling:	10,800 m (DIS), 9,800 m (DIS-T)
Rate of climb:	5'30" (DIS) 6'18" (DIS-T)
Range:	2280 kms (DIS), 2500 kms (DIS-T)
Armament (DIS):	1 x 30 mm VYa MK, 2 x 12.7 mm UBK MK, 4 x 7.62 mm ShKAS MG and up to one tonne additional load (planned)
Additional payload:	1 to 2 x 30 mm VYa MK, 2 x 12.7 mm UBK MG, 4 x 7.62 mm ShKAS MG

and the works did not have the capacity for a series run. Therefore the possibilities of the two aircraft were never examined and were eventually overtaken.

Under the direction of Pietr D. Grushin at OKO-1, the two-engined escort fighter DIS equipped with Mikulin AM-37 V-motors in the summer of 1940. (Georg Mader)

The second prototype DIS-T with Shvetzov M-82F radial motors was seen as a fighter- and torpedo-bomber.

MiG-6

In July 1940, two months after work began on its predecessor PBSh-1, OKO-1 began developing the PBSh-2, also known as the MiG-6. This ground-attack aircraft prototype was smaller, and designed as a single-seat biplane with swept-forward wings, the lower wing being larger than the upper. Shafts for small bombs were planned to be fitted on the inner wing of the lower surface and the armoured cockpit had a side-door removable by an explosive charge. This second ground-attack project was also abandoned at the end of 1940.

Aircraft type:	MiG-6
Purpose:	Ground attack aircraft prototype
Crew:	1
Engine plant:	1 x Mikulin AM-38 V-12 engine 1600 hp (planned)
Wingspan:	upper wing 8.6 m; lower wing 12.4 m. Length 8.85 m, Wing area, 32.4 sq.m
Take-off weight:	max, 4828 kgs
Top speed:	(ground level): 426 kms/hr estimated
Ceiling:	7600 m estimated
Range:	740 kms estimated
Armament:	2 x 23 mm VJ 23 MK with 96 rounds each, 6 x 7.62 mm ShKAS MG each with 750 rounds, up to 500 kg bombload

The I-230 was a further development of the MiG-3 from 1942 (Jerzy Butkiewicz).

I-230

The I-230 project was a further development of the MiG-3 with better aerodynamics and other modifications, parts of the MiG-3 being included in the structure. Because the planned 12-cylinder V-motor Mikulin AM-39 was not yet available, and the AM-38F was reserved for the Ilyushin Il-2, the I-230 received the same engine plant as the MiG-3, the Mikulin AM-35A. From this came the MiG-3U (=improved) and D (=long range). The maiden flight of the first I-230 prototype took place on 11 August 1942, but as the production of the Mikulin AM-35A motor was suspended, series production of the MiG-3U did not proceed. There was a pre-series run of five aircraft which eventually became operational on the Kalinin Front.

Top: As the Mikulin AM-39 engine was not ready, and the AM-38F not available in sufficient quantities, there was no series run of the I-230.

Aircraft type:	I-230
Purpose:	Fighter prototype
Crew:	1
Engine plant:	1 x Mikulin AM 35A 12-cylinder V-engine, 1350 hp. Wingspan 10.20 m (Nr.1), 11 m (Nr 2). Length, 8.62 m
Wing area:	17.44 sq.m (Nr 1) 18 sq.m (Nr 2)
Weight empty:	2612 kgs, max
Take-off weight:	3285 kgs
Top speed:	(low level): 560 kms/hr, (6,000 m) 660 kms/hr
Ceiling:	11500 m (Nr 1), 12,000 m (Nr 2)
Rate of climb to 5,000 m:	6 mins 12 secs
Range:	1300 kms
Armament:	2 x 20 mm ShVAK-20 MK, 150 rounds each

The I-230 was a further development of the MiG-3 from 1942.

I-211

In February 1942 the Soviet Air Force chiefs decided to develop a variant of the MiG-3/M-82 with a radial motor suitable for use at the front, project code E(Ye). OKB 155 (MiG) received the support of the TsAGI (Central Institute for Aero- and Hydrodynamics) and the Arkadia D. Shvetzov design bureau for the project. The 14-cylinder double radial Shvetzov ASh-82FN engine for the I-211 based on the MiG-3 was identical to the Lavotshkin La-5, but necessitated a complete reworking of the MiG-3 fuselage. First flight of the I-211 took place on 18 December 1942 and on subsequent flight tests it proved so extraordinarily manoevrable that according to contemporary reports it banked better than any existing Soviet fighters. There was no factory capacity for the series production of this fighter, also known as the MiG-9, and only a pre-series of ten was built, these operating on the Kalinin Front from September 1943.

The lack of engines for the MiG-3 led to the I-211, an alternative variant with a Shvetzov M-82FN radial motor.

Aircraft type:	I.211
Purpose:	Fighter prototype
Crew:	1
Engine plant:	1 x Shvetzov M-82FN (Ash-82 FN) 14 cylinder double radial engine, 1650 hp
Wingspan:	10.2 m, length 7.95 m
Wing area:	17.44 sq.m
Weight empty:	2528 kgs, max
Take-off weight:	3100 kgs
Top speed:	(7,000 m) 670 kms/hr
Ceiling:	11,300 m
Rate of climb:	(5000 m) 4 mins
Range:	1140 kms
Armament:	2 x 20mm ShVAK-20 MK, 150 rounds each

Although the I-211 had good flying qualities, series production was not possible for lack of production capacity during the winter of 1942.

I-231

At the end of 1942 work began on the high-altitude I-231, project code 2D – unofficially also known as the MiG-3DD – to be fitted with the new Mikulin AM-39A 1900 hp engine. Maiden flight was in February 1943, and in subsequent tests at NII (Scientific Research Institute) the aircraft was wrecked in a crash. Because the new AM-39A engine was not yet ready for series production and there was no capacity for a series run, the I-231 was the only one of its kind.

Aircraft type:	I-231
Purpose:	High-altitude aircraft prototype
Crew:	1
Engine plant:	1 x Mikulin AM-39A 12-cylinder V-motor, 1900 hp
Wingspan:	10.2 m, length 8.62 m
Wing area:	17.44 sq m
Weight empty:	2583 kgs
Max take-off weight:	3287 kgs
Top speed:	(7100 m) 707 kms/hr
Ceiling:	11,400 m
Rate of climb:	(5000 m) 4 mins 30 secs
Range:	1140 kms
Armament:	2 x 20mm ShVAK-20 MK each with 160 rounds

The high altitude fighter I-231 was flight tested in February 1943 (Dipl.Ing. Jerzy Butkiewicz).

The I-231 was abandoned after the prototype crashed and the Mikulin AM-39A motor intended for it was not ready for full production.

I-220

At the beginning of 1941, OKB 155 (MiG) was given orders to build a high altitude interceptor, this being project A of the prototype I-220. As the first Mikoyan-Gurevitch machine, the I-220 was given a large wingspan with a laminary profile developed by the Central Institute for Aero- and Hydrodynamics. The I-220 fuselage was longer than that of the MiG-3. It was originally intended to fit the I-220 with a Mikulin AM-39A V-motor, but as it was not ready in time a 1700 hp AM-38F engine was mounted in the first prototype. The first take-offs took place at the beginning of July 1943, for the rest of the summer the aircraft was tested at the Scientific Research Institute and received the designation MiG-11. In January 1944 the I-220 returned to OKB 155 to be fitted with the Mikulin AM 39A motor. In the third week of that month there was another series of tests with the I-220(1). The second

Aircraft type:	I-220(2)
Purpose:	Fighter prototype
Crew:	1
Engine plant:	1 x Mikulin AM-39A V-112 motor, 1900 hp
Wingspan:	11 m, length 9.6 m
Wing area:	20.38 sq.m
Weight empty:	3101 kgs
Max take-off weight:	3647 kgs
Top speed:	(ground level) 572 kms/hr (7000 m) 697 kms/hr
Ceiling:	11,000 m
Rate of climb (6000 m):	4 mins 30 secs
Range:	630 kms
Armament:	4 x 20 mm ShVAK-20 MK, 2 (150 rounds) each side of motor, 2 (100 rounds) above

prototype received the same engine plant upon completion and I-220(2) was tested as from the beginning of September 1944. It was planned to install a turbocharger in the second prototype, but by the autumn of 1944 the machine was already obsolescent.

The high altitude fighter I-220 took off for the first time in July 1943 (Dipl.Ing. Jerzy Butkiewicz).

Trials of the second I-220 prototype began in September 1944. There was no series run, for by then the type was already obsolescent (Butkiewicz).

I-221

In 1943 work on Project 2A, a high altitude interceptor based on the MiG-3, was begun. This aircraft was an answer to the new German high-level bomber/reconnaissance Ju 388K and L, which could fly at altitudes of around 13,000 metres. To some extent I-221 was similar to I-220, but had 2 metres wider wingspan. Engine plant was a Mikulin AM-39A V-motor. The I-221 was the first OKB 155 (MiG) aircraft to receive two TK-2B turbochargers, but for reasons of space the designers were forced to abandon the originally planned heavy ShVAK machine-cannons and settle instead for the weaker variation fitted to the earlier MiG fighters. The first flight by the prototype took place on 2 December 1943. The designation MiG-7 was suggested for the series run. After the first test flights it was apparent that a pressure cabin and machine-cannons were imperative. On the first test flight after these modifications a connecting rod in the engine broke and the I-

221 crashed. Project 2A was not pursued after that although the experience gained flowed into the development of the succeeding prototypes I-222 and I-224.

Aircraft type:	I-221
Purpose:	High altitude aircraft prototype
Crew:	1
Engine plant:	1 x Mikulin AM-39A 12-cylinder V-motor with two TK-2B turbochargers and 1900 hp take-off thrust
Wingspan:	13 m, length 9.55m
Wing area:	22.44 sq.m
Weight empty:	3179 kgs
Max take-off weight:	3888 kgs
Top speed:	(7000 m) 689 kms/hr
Ceiling:	13,000 to 14,500 m
Rate of climb (5000 m):	4 mins 36 secs
Range:	1000 kms
Armament:	1 x 12.7 mm UBS MG, 2 x 7.62 mm ShKAS MG
Armament:	2 x 20 mm ShVAK-20 MK, 150 rounds each

The I-221 reached a maximum ceiling of 14,500 m. (Butkiewicz)

I-222

Based on the I-221, the high altitude fighter prototype I-222, project code 3A, flew on 7 May 1944 for the first time. The aircraft had a wooden fuselage, a TK-300B turbocharger and a pressure cabin. It was thought it would enter series production as MiG-7. Although the war situation had changed and the Soviet Air Force no longer had an urgent need for a machine of this type, the development was continued to its conclusion and then abandoned.

Aircraft type:	I-222
Purpose:	High altitude aircraft prototype
Crew:	1
Engine plant:	1 x Mikulin AM-39B-1 12-cylinder V-motor with one TK-300b turbocharger, 1900 hp take-off thrust
Wingspan:	13 m, length 9.6 m
Wing area:	22.44 sq.m
Weight empty:	3167 kgs
Max take-off weight:	3790 kgs
Top speed:	(6700 m) 682 kms/hr, (13,100 m) 691 kms/hr
Ceiling:	14,500 m
Rate of climb:	(5000 m) 5 mins 30 secs
Range:	1000 kms
Armament:	2 x 20mm ShVAK-20 MK, 80 rounds each

Because the Soviet Air Force had no need for a high altitude fighter in 1944 given the war situation, the I-222 was not series produced.

Based on the I-221, the high altitude fighter prototype I-222 with a turbocharger made its appearance in the spring of 1944.

I-225

The prototype I-225, project code 5A, combined the special properties of a high altitude aircraft with those of a fighter for the intermediate heights. The powerful Mikulin AM 42 motor made the two I-225 prototypes not only into the fastest piston-driven aircraft in the Soviet Union, but also gave a satisfactory performance and had a greater range than all previous single-engined MiG fighters. Both versions of the Mikulin AM-42 motor could be fitted with a TK-300B turbocharger if desired. The maiden flight of the first prototype I-225-01, fitted with a 2000 hp AM-42B motor, took place on 21 July 1944, but on the fifteenth test flight the aircraft was damaged. The second prototype I-225-02 with an AM-42FB engine flew for the first time on 14 March 1945. Because the need for a high-altitude piston-driven fighter no longer existed, there was no series production.

Aircraft type:	I-225
Purpose:	Fighter prototype
Crew:	1
Engine plant:	1 x Mikulin AM-42B 12-cylinder V-motor, 2000 hp (I-225-01): 1 x Mikulin AM-42FB 12-cylinder V-motor, 1900 hp (I-225-02)
Wingspan:	11 m, length 9.6 m
Wing area:	20.38 sq.m
Weight empty:	3010 kgs
Max take-off weight:	3900 kgs
Top speed:	(low level) 617 kms/hr (8500 m) 720 kms/hr
Ceiling:	12,600 m
Rate of climb (5000 m):	4 mins 30 secs
Range:	1300 kms
Armament:	4 x 20 mm ShVAK-20 MK, 100 rounds each

The I-225 was conceived as a fighter for intermediate and great altitudes and proved to be the fastest piston-driven aircraft in the Soviet Union (Butkiewicz).

The second I-225 prototype flew for the first time in March 1945, but by then was already absolete, for jet fighters were now seen as the aircraft of the future (Butkiewicz).

I-224

Project 4A, begun in 1943, was a high-altitude aircraft for 14,000 m, based on the I-221 but driven by a Mikulin AM39B motor with TK-300B turbocharger, the propellor being the four-bladed paddle type. With about the same take-off weight as the I-221, the I-224 had better horizontal and climb characteristics than the predecessor. I-224 was the last OKB 155 piston-driven high altitude aircraft. Assembled in the summer of 1944, it flew for the first time on 20 October. On the first test flights unpleasantly strong vibrations from the compressor wheels of the turbocharger were felt at 24,000 revs/min. On a subsequent test flight one of the compressor wheels burst apart as the result of materials failure causing an engine explosion. After this setback, completion of the second prototype was cancelled on the grounds that the next model, I-225 had not yet flown and the work on the great hope I-250 with mixed propulsion outstripped OKB 155 capacity. As for I-221 and I-222, I-224 was to have been given the designation MiG-7, later changed to MiG-11, but no series production ensued for any of them.

Aircraft type:	I-224
Purpose:	High-altitude aircraft prototype
Crew:	1
Engine plant:	1 x Mikulin AM-42FB V-12 with TK-300B turbocharger, 1750 hp take-off performance
Wingspan:	13 m, length 9.51 m
Wing area:	22.44 sq.m
Wheelbase:	3.65 m
Weight empty:	3105 kgs
Max take-off weght:	3921 kgs
Top speed:	(low level) 601 kms/hr (13,100 m) 693 kms/hr
Ceiling:	14,100 m
Rate of climb (5000 m):	4 mins 48 secs, Range, more than 1000 kms (estimated)
Armament:	2 x 20mm ShVAK-20 MK, 100 rounds each

The second I-224 prototype was never completed after an engine explosion due to materials failure which occurred during a test flight of the original.

The I-224 was the last high altitude piston-engined design of the OKB 155 (MiG) (Butkiewicz).

MiG-13

When the first German jet aircraft appeared, the Soviet leadership did everything it could to develop a Soviet jet in order to combat the new threat as soon as possible. On Stalin's direct order, which reproached the Soviet aeronautical industry for not having developed a home-grown jet of its own, in March 1944 the design bureaux of Mikoyan-Gurevitch and Pavel Sukhoi set to work on a jet-fighter emergency programme whose primary aim was the highest possible speed attainable.

At this time the Soviet Union had only the VRD-2 jet turbine, which Archip Lyulka had begun developing at the beginning of 1943 but was still in the testing stage. This turbine did not create the thrust to propel a fighter, making the installation of a conventional piston-engine necessary. OKN 155 (MiG) met this challenge with the I-250 prototype, project N, while at OKB Sukhoi began work on the prototype I-107, the later Sukhoi Su-5.

Aircraft type	MiG-13
Purpose:	Fighter
Crew:	1
Engine plant:	1 x Klimov VK-107R V12 motor, max 1650 hp and VRDK compressor, 1350 hp
Wingspan:	9.5 m, length 8.18 m
Wing area:	15 sq.m
Weight empty:	3028 kgs
Max take-off weight:	3931 kgs
Top speed:	(low level) 620 kms/hr (7000 m) 825 kms/hr
Ceiling:	10,500 m without compressor, 11,960 m with compressor
Rate of climb (5,000 m):	3 mins 54 secs (with compressor)
Range:	920 kms (with compressor), 1380 kms (without compressor)
Armament:	3 x 20mm Beresin B-20 MK, 160 rounds each

The I-250-01 was fitted with a Klimov VK-107R V-motor and a VRDK compressor, which provided in parallel 3000 hp.

Because the VRD-2 was not yet available, OKB MiG suggested for the I-250 another combination. The main drive would be a Klimov VK-107R with propellor and a VRDK compressor. This device, under development at the Central Institute for Aircraft Engine Design (TsIAM) since 1942, had the same fuel as was injected into the VK-107R motor. A gas exhaust at the rear of the I-250 provided the aircraft with an additional 300 kgs thrust. On 26 October 1944 a mock-up of the I-250 was put together and the first prototype N-1 (I-250-01) flew for the first time on 3 March 1945. With effect from the third test flight, the VRDK compressor was connected at

The I-250-02 suffered the same fate as the first prototype and was destroyed during trials.

00 kms/hr, and although this had only ten minutes running time, the N-1 reached a maximum speed of 825 kms/hr at 7,000 metres ith the joint thrust of 3,000 hp. On 19 May 945 the N-1 crashed as the result of structural ilure under high G-stresses, and the second rototype (I-250-02) was also wrecked while naking an emergency landing during trials. naware of these setbacks, in July 1945 the oviet Air Force instructed OKB 155 (MiG) to repare ten examples of the I-250 by the oming 7 November for a demonstration flight to be witnessed by heads of the Soviet Government. Throwing everything into the job and working round the clock, OKB succeeded in building nine of these fighters ready to fly with this mixed propulsion by the deadline – and then the fly-past was cancelled because of inclement weather.

By 1946 another sixteen I-250's were built and received the official designation MiG-13. These fighters were similar to the I-250-02 and all sixteen MiG-13's of the series production were delivered to the Soviet Air Force.

Because the Soviet leaders placed great value on a fighter with a modern propulsion system, in 1946 a small eries of MiG-13's was manufactured.

MiG-8 "Utka"

Under the directorship of Colonel G. A. Tokayev at OKB 155 (MiG), in 1945 students at the Shukovski Air Force Academy designed an experimental aircraft with duck wings, pressure propellor and a fixed undercarriage which received the designation MiG-8 "Utka" (duck). It was hoped to obtain new experience from this aircraft for future jet types. At the rear of the machine was a 110 hp 5-cylinder Shvetzov M-11F radial motor driving a two-bladed wooden propellor. The maiden flight was made on 19 November 1945 and after minor problems had been resolved by a number of modifications, Utka proved itself to be an extraordinarily stable design. After its testing, Utka remained in service for many years as the OKB 155 firm's aircraft.

The MiG-8 was a purely experimental aircraft and served subsequently for many years as the OKB-1 firm's aircraft.

The maiden flight of the Utka was made in winter conditions.

Aircraft type:	MiG-8 "Utka"
Purpose:	Experimental aircraft
Crew:	1
Engine:	1 x 5-cylinder radial Schvetzov M-11F, 110 hp
Wingspan:	9.5 m, length 6.99 m
Wing area:	15 sq.m
Weight empty:	642 kgs
Max take-off weight:	1150 kgs
Top speed:	205 kms/hr
Range:	500 kms, no armament

The MiG-8 Utka was built in 1945 at OKB-155 (MiG) by students of the Shukovski Air Force Academy.

MiG-9

Resulting from the demands of the Soviet Air Force generals for jet aircraft, in February 1945 work also began at OKB 155 (MiG) on a single-seater jet fighter. The design of the I-300 was all-metal and initially it was planned to fit two copied BMW 003A turbines each with 800 kp thrust in gondolas beneath the wings. After various calculations and wind-tunnel experiments the two engines were situated side-by-side in the fuselage so that the aircraft could fly on one alone. At the end of December 1945 the mainframe of the first prototype I-

Aircraft type:	MiG-9
Purpose:	Fighter
Crew:	1
Engine plant:	2 x RD-20F (BMW 003A) 880 kp thrust each
Wingspan:	10 m, length 9.83 m, he. 3.25 m
Wing area:	18.32 sq.m
Weight empty:	3420 kgs
Max take-off weight:	4963 kgs
Top speed (5,000 m):	910 kms/hr
Ceiling:	13,000 m
Armament:	1 x 37mm NS-37 MK, 40 rounds: 2 x 23mm NS MK, each 80 rounds
Additional payload:	2 x 235 litre outboard tar

The MiG-9 caused a sensation upon its introduction to the public during the Tushino air show on 18 August 1946.

The MiG-9FR was a modified version with more powerful turbines and different armament.

300 was completed and in March of the following year the first prototype I-300F-1 was rolled out of the hangar and transferred to the flight testing centre of the Scientific Research Institute NII at Chalovskaya. There the Mikoyan-Gurevitch team met that of OKB Yakovlev which was testing the competitor design Yak-15.

On 24 April 1946 the I-300 F-1 took off on its maiden flight and thus became the first jet to be flown by the Soviet Union. The flight of the Yak-15 followed three hours later from the same airfield. On later test flights at speeds of over 750 kms/hr heavy vibrations were reported. These were cured by strengthening the rudder assembly and boarding over the underside with stainless steel. Subsequently the I-300 F-1 reached a speed of 911 kms/hr at 4,500 metres without problems.

An unexpected end arrived on the 19th test flight on 11 July 1946 when I-300F-1 suddenly stood on its nose at 200 metres altitude, turned a somersault and exploded on contact with the ground, killing the pilot.

Two further prototypes had been completed meanwhile and fitted with RD-20F engines. The third prototype I-300F-3, which flew for the first time on 9 August 1946, carried out high speed flight tests, while the second prototype I-300F-2, maiden flight 11 August 1946, flew at slow speeds and also on only one turbine. After further test flights in which near-crash situations were observed, the trials were finally ended at the end of August 1946 and the type declared ready for series production, just at the right moment for its presentation to the public on the occasion of the great Soviet Air Force airshow at Tushino on 18 August. The Mikoyan-Gurevitch MiG-9 jet was a sensation and even Stalin was so impressed that he ordered a formation of fifteen MiG-9's to take part in the fly-past at the Anniversary Parade of the October Revolution on Red Square the coming 7 November.

The I-302(FP) was a prototype with a repositioning of its cannons.

At the beginning of 1946 a two-seater training version was ordered, which resulted in the MiG-9UTI.

The K-1 was a manned test version of the air-to-ground guided weapon KS-1, also designed by OKB 155 (MiG

This requirement was almost impossible to meet, for there were neither fittings nor moulds ready for series production of the MiG-9 and the available drawings were only of the prototypes. The aircraft known only as I-301 had a longer nose and other modifications as compared to the I-300 prototype. When Mikoyan was received at the Kremlin he was given to understand that he had no great future if he failed to comply with the wish of the dictator. Thus the fifteen machines were worked at

around-the-clock, which also meant that about 60,000 works drawings had to be turned out. After four weeks' stress and strain the first MiG-9 was completed. The others followed and on 15 October 1946 the fifteenth and last was ready to take off. Ironically – as with the MiG-13 a year before – all the effort was in vain for on the "Day of the October Revolution" thick fog enshrouded Red Square and all planned fly-pasts had to be cancelled. The presentation of the fifteen jets was postponed until the May

Day celebrations, 1947. The same year the air force began training its pilots on the MiG-9.

At the beginning of 1946, to improve flight training for future MiG-9 single-seater fighters, a two-seater training version was requested. The two prototypes I-301T of the future UTI MiG-9 and MiG-9UTI with dual controls were given the project codes F-1 and

The MiG-9L "Laboratoriya" was a one-off to test the guidance system of the KS-1 "Kometa" air-to-ground guided missile (Butkiewicz).

FT-2. FT-1 flew for the first time in July 1947 fitted with BMW 003A turbines. The maiden flight of the second machine followed on 25 August of the same year. Both cockpits had ejector seats and the FT-2 was the first aircraft in the Soviet Union from which a pilot could be catapulted free. Because of the repeated engine failures caused by the gases given off when the NS-37 cannon mounted in the partition bulkhead of the air intake was fired at altitudes above 7,500 metres, the I-302(P) was a modified version with the 37mm cannon repositioned to the upper left of the nose. This solution was not continued in the series.

The MiG-9FR(I-308) which appeared in 1946 was a version with the more powerful RD-21 turbines each providing 950 kp of thrust. The pressure cabin was located a little farther forward making necessary a change in the armament. The principal variant of the I-308 was to have been the MiG-9M but was soon dropped in favour of the much more promising I-310 – the later MiG-15. The prototype for a single jet variant of the MiG-9 was designated I-305 and also FL (F-Lyulka) but on account of the I-310 this project was also abandoned before the maiden flight. The I-307 (FF) had RD-20F engines with after-burners, and extra armour and flew for the first time in September 1947. This machine, known to Western authors as the MiG-9FF, received the nickname "Babutshka" (butterfly) but remained a one-off. The I-320 (FN) was to have received a Rolls-Royce Nene turbine but the plan was given up in mid-1947. Later an experimental machine, MiG-9PB, was converted to try out slippertanks under the wings. Another one-off was the MiG-9L "Laboratoriya" for the FK (F-Comet) project, also known as MiG-9UTI-LL or UTI MiG-9LL "Letayushchaya Laboratoriya" (flying

laboratory), to test the guidance system for the KS-1 air-to-ground guided missile. The KS-1 was a development of the SB-1 from OKB 155 (MiG) and known in the West as AS-1 "Kennel". For its role as a flying laboratory the MiG-9L received a substantial conversion in which the fuselage was lengthened to accommodate a second cockpit and various internal aerials. Besides the

This MiG-9 is at the Soviet Air Force museum, Monino. (Georg Mader)

"Laboratoriya", to test the KS-1, a K-1 KSK – a manned version of the guided missile – was built. K-1 had a 10-metre wingspan, an overall length of 10.12 metres, a wing area of 18.2 square metres and performed like a smaller MiG-15.

Meanwhile the Air Standards Coordinating Committee had given the MiG-9 the codename "Fargo" and in the course of 1947 the aircraft was delivered to the fighter squadrons of the Soviet Air Force, its numbers quickly increasing for the ground-attack role. The Mikoyan-Gurevitch MiG-9 was in service for only a few years with the Soviet Air Force, however, being replaced in 1949 with the much more efficient MiG-15.

I-270

After the Red Army captured two Messerschmitt Me 163B rocket aircraft of the German Luftwaffe at the beginning of 1944, OKB 155 (MiG) was requested to see if this aircraft type could be reproduced with a Dushkin-Glushko rocket motor. No prototype was built, but after the design bureau received data of the Me 263/Junkers Ju 248 programmes including a prototype after the war, the Soviet leadership decided that OKB 155 should build a similar machine. A Ju 248 served as the basis for the I-270 prototype, project code Zh, but more streamlined, with larger rudder gear and non-swept wings. The robust landing gear had great similarity to that of the Ju 248. The first

Aircraft type:	I-270
Purpose:	Fighter-prototype
Crew:	1
Engine plant:	1 x Dushkin/Glushko RD-2M-3V rocket motor, 1450 kgs thrust (only Zh-2)
Wingspan:	7.75m, length 8.91 m
Wing area:	12 sq.m
Weight empty:	1546 kgs
Max take-off weight:	4120 kgs
Top speed:	(low level) 1000 kms/hr (5,000 m) 900 kms/hr (10,000 m) 928 kms/hr (15,000 m) 936 kms/hr. Ceiling 17,000 m
Rate of climb to 10,000 m:	2 mins 37 secs
Armament:	2 x 23 mm NS -23 MK, 40 rounds each, 8 x RS 82 rockets

Based on captured Me 263 files, in 1946 the rocket-propelled I-270 appeared (Hans-Jürgen Becker).

The first prototype was a pure glider, the second I-270 received an RD-2M-3V rocket motor.

Zh-prototype was completed as a glider without engine plant and tested from December 1946, towed by a Tupolev Tu-2. The second prototype was given an RD-2M-3V rocket motor with 1450 kgs thrust developed by Dushkin and Glushko. The Zh-2 had an ejector seat and was armed with two NS-23 machine-cannons. In March 1947 the second I-270 displayed poor manoevrability in trials while range was very short with a 4 minute 15 second burn. OKB 155 saw no more development potential in the type and the upset was not great when the Zh-2 undercarriage was damaged during a hard landing and the Zh-1 glider was not repaired after a belly landing.

MiG-15

In 1946, the Soviet leadership asked for a new jet fighter to incorporate the most recent experience of high speed flight, reach a speed of 0.9 Mach and be able to take off from unmade air strips. Furthermore the aircraft had to be very nimble at altitudes above 11,000 metres and able to stay up for at least an hour. All fighter designers of the time were co-opted to assist in this project. In cooperation with the Central Institute for Aero- and Hydrodynamics TsAGI, the various bureaus submitted studies on all kinds of swept wings, including forward-swept wings, as in the Tsybin S. project. Because the latest available swept-wing studies in the Soviet Union dated back to 1935, the designers had much work confronting them.

After a Soviet Commission bought Rolls-Royce Nene engines in Great Britain in the autumn of 1946, in February 1947 OKB 155

Aircraft type:	MiG-15bis
Purpose:	Fighter
Crew:	1
Engine plant:	1 x Klimov VK-1 turbojet, 2700 kgs thrust
Wingspan:	10.08 m, length 10.10 m
Wing area:	20.6 sq.m
Weight empty:	3681 kgs
Max take-off weight:	5055 kgs
Top speed:	(low level) 1076 kms/hr (3000 m) 1107 kms/hr (5000 m) 1014 kms/hr
Ceiling:	15,500 m
Rate of climb (5,000 m):	1 min 57 secs (10,000 m) 4 mins 54 secs
Climb performance:	46m/sec
Range:	1330 kms (with outboard tanks)
Armament:	1 x 37mm N37 MK, 40 rounds, 2 x 23mm NS-23 MK, 2 x 100 kg FAB-100 bombs

After the 1956 uprising in Hungary, the country lost the trust of the Kremlin and for many years subsequently had to make do with older military materials.

At the beginning of 1949 the first MiG-15's were delivered to the Soviet Air Force (Georg Mader).

(MiG) received from the design bureau of Vladimir Klimov exact technical specifications of this engine, designated RD-45 in the Soviet Union, which was to be mounted in a fighter aircraft then under development, project code S (strelovidnost=swept), given the number I-310 by the Scientific Research Institute NII. The first prototype S-01 was completed on 27 November 1947 and first flew on 30 December. Some minor modifications were carried out in the following months and the second prototype S-02 flew for the first time on 27 May 1948. This machine had been given a powerful Nene-2 turbine with 2200 kgs thrust, an S-13 film camera above the nose and small smoke-making rockets were fixed below the wings to observe better the tailspin propensity. The third prototype S-03 was completed in March 1948, all recognised disadvantages having been removed. On 17 June 1948 the S-03 made its

maiden flight. Despite an unsatisfactory flight attitude at great altitude and a tendency to enter a tailspin when banking to the right, the S-03 reached Mach 0.91/0.92 and proved itself superior to all competing designs. Therefore in August 1948 project S was accepted for series production as the MiG-15.

The first MiG-15 series, also designated SV (swept air-wing) and propelled by a Klimov RD-45 jet engine, was built at GAZ-1 (National Aircraft factory) and received a number of improvements over the succeeding months. The first MiG-15's were delivered primarily to technical units, to the Soviet Naval-Air Force AV-MF and Air Defence Command PVO founded on 8 October 1948. During this period of deliveries modifications to the MiG-15 continued and thus amongst other changes the more powerful Klimov RD-45F was introduced with 2270 kgs thrust. Initially the designations

"Jaguar" and "Sas" (eagle) were used for this aircraft in the East, but did not persist.

On 20 May 1949 the Politburo decided for the series production of the MiG-15 as the most important new fighter aircraft of the Soviet Air Force and as a result the series runs of the competitor models Yak-17, Yak-23 and La-15, and the transport Li-2 were abandoned. Licences to reproduce the MiG-15 design were also conferred on Czechoslovakia as S-102 and S-103, on PZL Mielec in Poland as LiM 1 and on the People's Republic of China as J-2 (Jianjiji=fighter) and F-2. The LiM-1 had improved navigational and radio equipment and was known as LiM-1.5. By 1956 a total of about 12,000 MiG-15's had been built, about half as the two-seater trainer MiG-15UTI. When the MiG-15 first appeared over Korea in November 1950, the performance of this aircraft came as a great shock for the West. Initially the Air Standards Coordinating Committee (ASCC) awarded the MiG-15 the code "Falcon", but then they thought that was

The MiG-15 was produced under licence in China and Poland, and as S-102 shown here in the Czech Soviet Socialist Republic.

too flattering and changed it to "Faggot-A" instead. During the testing of the first prototype S-01 in 1947 the need for a dual-seat training version was recognised but OKB 155 did not receive the development order until 13 April 1949. The two-seater MiG-15UTI was identical to the single seater except for the front end of the fuselage. Because the rear cockpit limited the fuel capacity inside the aircraft to 1,120 litres, two outboard tanks each with 280 or 400 litres capacity were developed for the trainer. The armament of the UTI, not mounted aboard every machine but which was easy to install and remove, consisted of a single NR-23 machine-cannon. The UTI prototype, known at the works as project ST, made its maiden flight on 23 May 1949 and the testing of the aircraft, designated I-312 by the Scientific Research Institute NII, lasted until May 1950. Production of the MiG-15UTI under licence followed in Czechoslovakia as CS-102, in Poland as LiM-3 and in China as JJ-2, also FT-2. A two-seater operational variant of the UTI with an AFA-21 and AFA-39 aerial film camera was built as LiM-2A and LiM-2R respectively with two AFA-40 cameras for the Polish Air Force. Another Polish modification of the UTI as a two-seater reconnaissance and artillery spotter aircraft with an AFA-21 aerial camera was the LiM 1A. Throughout the entire period of production new varieties of cockpit instrumentation continued to appear and from the fourth completion block the two-seaters lost the cannon armament altogether. One of these modified UTI's was the protoype ST-2 with a smaller fuselage tank, tested with various new cockpit instruments. ASCC called the MiG-15UTI "Midget". From 1952 every fighter regiment of the Soviet Air Force had, besides its Mig-15

The Hungarian Air Force also received the single- and dual seater MiG-15. (Laszlo Javor)

single seaters, four MiG-15UTI's as a permanent feature of pilot training, used in later years for conversion training to the MiG-17 and MiG-19. In 1953 the prototype ST-7 of the "radar-trainer" MiG-15UTI-P made its debut. The next development stage of the MiG-15 fighter began as project SD, substantially revised and fitted with a Klimov VK-1 engine, a further development of the RD-45 turbine. Although the first flight of this aircraft known as a MiG-15bis took place in September 1949, the production of the modified type did not begin until 1952. As with the predecessor, the MiG-15bis ("Faggot-B") was built under licence in Czechoslovakia as S-102 and in Poland as LiM-2. In the same year the development stage of the MiG-17 began with two prototypes MiG-15bis-45° and MiG-15strela-45° which had a greater sweep to the wings and were also known as SI-2 and SI-3.

In order to solve the inherent control problems of the MiG-15 at high altitude, a research group was set up at OKB MiG in the first half of 1949 for the purpose. Two aircraft of the series run were made available for experimental work. Both machines were designated SE ("swept wing special") and "flying laboratory", also MiG-15UTI-LL or UTI MiG-15 LL. In order to better control yaw the rudder and aileron surfaces were enlarged. Test flights began in July 1949, on 21 September that year a speed of Mach 0.985 was reached and after further modifications on 21 September the sound barrier was broken at Mach 1.01.

In the following December, testing of the Torjii radar for an all-weather version began aboard the SP-1, MiG-15P and MiG-15bis. The on-board radar RP-1 Izumrud (Smaragd) proved more efficient, however, and from the

The arrival of the MiG-15 on the scene and its performance capabilities came as an unpleasant surprise for the Western air forces. (Georg Mader)

MiG-15UTI (in this photo in Finnish Air Force livery) was the version of the MiG-15 to remain in operational service longest, being used in many countries as a training aircraft for the next generation of MiG pilots.

beginning of 1950 was fitted in a radar dome above the air intake of a MiG-15 of the series production designated as SP-5. From 1951 five more aircraft of the series were made available for the further development of on-board radar, these being designated MiG-15bisP. Other versions were the MiG-15R as a photo reconnaissance aircraft, the MiG-15S as an escort fighter with supplementary tanks, the MiG-15SW as a high-altitude escort fighter with powerful cannons, the MiG-15SB as a fighter-bomber operating from unpaved airfields and the MiG-15T to tow target drogues. In 1950 the grotesque experimental MiG-15 "Burlaki" appeared fitted with a compressed air cannon in the nose able to fire a harpoon enabling it to link up with a friendly bomber in flight and be towed by this bomber over long distances as a glider. The idea was that the "Burlaki" would provide fighter cover for Soviet long range bombers beyond the normal fighter range. Strange though the concept may sound, it was

practicable, for there exists film of Burlakis being towed by other MiG-15's.

From 1950 there appeared, based on the MiG-15bis, also the MiG-15bisS (MiG-15Sbis) for escort duties, the MiG-15Fbis for fighter reconnaissance, the MiG-15bisF with a fixed inbuilt camera, MiG-15bisR with two AFA-40 cameras and the MiG-15Pbis and MiG-15bisP as a radar-equipped interceptor. The variants MiG-15IShbis (MiG-15bisISh) and MiG-15SBbis (MiG-15bisSB) could be armed with bombs and rockets as ground attack aircraft. At the beginning of 1951 a MiG-15 was tested with new weapons under project codes U and SU. Instead of fixed machine cannons firing in the direction of travel, the prototype was given two gondolas at the chin whose two Shpitalni Sh-3 cannons, 115 rounds each, could be fired by a switch on the accelerator lever and the pilot's control stick over a field of fire of +11° to –7°. Trials showed however that for the efficiency of this weapons variant a much wider field of fire was necessary, and this led later to project SN on the MiG-17.

At the beginning of 1951 the experimental SD-21 appeared on the scene, this being basically a MiG-15bis with four wing stations, and about the same time trials began of the ST-7 of a MiG-15UTI, also known as UTI MiG-15P (interceptor trainer). Its RP-1 Izumrud radar was operated from the front seat by the flight instructor, and the armament consisted of two 12.7mm UBK E-machine guns below the nose. A small series of UTI MiG-15P was manufactured. The SB LiM, SB LiM 1A (SB LiM-1Art), SB LiM-2 and SB LiM-2A (SB LiM-1Art, SB LiM-2M) were MiG-15 UTI's completed at PZL Mielec, differing from each other as training, reconnaissance and artillery spotting aircraft by their technical equipment, armament and range.

The experimental SD-57 was another MiG-15 taken out of series production and converted into an attack aircraft. For this purpose the SD-57 at each of its wing pylons had a rocket launcher for twelve non-guided ARS-57 rockets. These tests led to twelve further Isch (Shturmovich).

In 1953 at least two MiG-15bis were fitted with fuel-tank sounding probes on top of the nose for air-to-air refuelling attempts with a Tupolev Tu-4N "Bull", and in 1955 a number of MiG-15's and MiG-15bis' were converted into remote-controlled drones designated SDK-5. The same year a MiG-15bis was converted into a remote-controlled guided weapon SDK-7 with a one tonne explosive payload.

A number of series versions and experimental aircraft of the MiG-15 were built. (Georg Mader)

I-320

In order to meet the demand made in January 1949 for a radar-equipped day-and-night fighter, OKB MiG developed project R based on the MiG-15 which received later from NII the designation I-320. It was planned that this aircraft would have the radar developed by the Slepushkin and Tikhomirov groups when it came into production. The three R prototypes looked like enlarged MiG-15's with a modified air intake and radar dome above it. R-1 made its maiden flight on 16 April 1949 and showed good characteristics although no radar was aboard. The R-2 flew in November that year propelled by a Klimov VK-1 turbojet and more powerful armament. Initially the R-2 had a Torjii radar installation and later its Korshun improvement. On 13 March 1950 a 37-mm round in one of the cannons exploded, but the damage was repaired by the 30th of the month. The third prototype flew for the first time the following day. The R-3 absorbed various improvements of its two predecessors and also had under each wing a 750-litre fuel tank which could be dropped using a small explosive charge. The Soviet Air Force preferred the twin-jet Yakovlev Yak-25 "Flashlight" as its all-weather interceptor fighter and the I-320 project was shelved. The three R-prototypes were used subsequently by OKB MiG for trials of the instrument landing system.

Aircraft type:	I-320
Purpose:	All-weather fighter prototype
Crew:	1
Engine plant:	1 x Klimov RD-45F jet, 2270 kgs thrust (R-1): 1 x Klimov VK-1 jet, 2700 kgs thrust (R-2 and R-3)
Wingspan:	14.2 m, length 15.77 m
Wing area:	41.2 sq.m
Weight empty:	7367 kgs (R-1), 7460 kgs, (R-2 and R-3)
Max take-off weight:	10265 kgs (R-1), 12095 kgs (R- and R-3)
Top speed:	(low level) 1040 kms/hr (R-2 and R-3), at 10000 m (all three) 994 kms/hr
Rate of climb:	(5000 m) 2 mins 18 secs (10000 m) 5 mins 39 secs
Climb performance:	46 m/sec
Range:	1,100 kms (R-1 without outboard tanks), 1950 kms (R-2 and R-3 with outboard tanks)
Armament:	2 x 37mm N37 MK (R-1), 3 x 37mm N-37 MK (R-2 and R-3

Initially a Torjil radar was mounted in the nose of the I-320 (Butkiewicz).

The I-320 (the photo shows the R-1) was an all-weather fighter based on the MiG-15. (Butkiewicz)

Only three I-320 prototypes were built (this is R-2), the Soviet Air Force preferring the Yakolev Yak-25 "Flashlight" as its all-weather and night-fighter.

MiG-17

In January 1949, scarcely five months before the MiG-15 was declared by the Politburo to be the most important modern fighter in the Soviet Union and cleared for mass production, OKB 155 (MiG) decided to begin work on a successor. Naturally the new project SI would if possible have all weaknesses of the predecessors eliminated. Approval for the development of the SI came in March 1949, and a prototype SI-1 was built for static testing, two others, SI-2 and SI-3 for flight tests. In the last week of December 1949 SI-2 was completed and flew for the first time on 13 January 1950. On 1 February the SI-2 reached a speed of 1,114 kms/hr in horizontal flight at 2,200 metres but crashed on 20 March. As the third prototype SI-3 never flew, two more prototypes, SI-01 and SI-02, were approved, SI-02 being completed and making the maiden

Aircraft type:	MiG-17PF
Purpose:	All-weather interceptor
Crew:	1
Engine plant:	1 x Klimov VK-1F turbojet, 2600 kgs thrust without afterburner, 3380 kgs with afterburner
Wingspan:	9.63m, length 11.68m, wing area 22.64 sq.m
Weight empty:	4182 kgs
Max take-off weight:	6280 kgs
Top speed:	(low level) 1050 kms/hr, (4000m) 1121 kms/hr **Ceiling:** 15,850 m
Climb performance:	55 m/sec
Range:	1000 kms
Armanent:	3 x 23 mm NR-23 MK, 100 rounds each

flight before the 01. Flight testing of both machines went off without incident and series production of the MiG-17 began on 1 September 1951.

MiG-17F's were in service with the air force of the German Democratic Republic between 1957 and 1985.

This MiG-17P "Warbird" photographed in the United States in 1995 wears North Vietnamese livery.

During production running improvements were made. In tests a speed of Mach 1.14 was attained on a slightly inclined flight path, and in April 1954 on a test flight the limit was pushed further to Mach 1.15.

Exports began in October 1952 and the aircraft received from ASCC the appelation "Fresco-A". In Hungary it was known as "Csuszo" (glider).

In the autumn of 1951 under project designation SF, the MiG-17F ("Fresco-C") received an afterburner. The first of these Klimov VK-1F turbojets was flight tested for the first time on 29 September 1951. Initially the afterburner only worked for three minutes below 7,000 metres altitude or for ten minutes higher up, but after improvements were made to the cooling and fuel supply system these limitations fell away. The squadrons received the first MiG 17F's in February 1953. Copies of the MiG-17F under licence soon followed in Poland as LiM-5, LiM-5F, LiM-5M, LiM 5P (ground attack aircraft with booster rockets and parachute canopy for take-off and landing respectively), LiM-5 MR (reconnaissance version of the LiM-5M), LiM-5R and LiM-6R (fighter reconnaissance) and LiM-6 (another version for close support and parachute braking), LiM-6bis (variant of the LiM-6 with adjustable swept-wings), LiM-6bisR (fighter reconnaissance version of the LiM-6bis). The experimental bomber LiM-6M was a development from a LiM-6P. In China MiG-17F's were copied by Shenjang as J-4 (F-4) and J-5. Because OKB was not offering a trainer version of the MiG-17, at Shenjang the cockpit of a MiG-15UTI was put into the mainframe of a MiG-17PF for their own two-seater version designated JJ-4, JJ-5, CJ-5 and HJ-5 and for export as F-5 and FT-5.

A MiG-17F was fitted out as the all-weather experimental SP-2, and besides other improvements received the Korshun radar. The SP-2 first flew on 11 March 1951 and between November and December of the same year went to the NII Scientific Research Institute for further appraisal. At the beginning of 1952 the latest development of the MiG-17P (SP-7) followed. This variant was conceived as a night- and all-weather interceptor, and ouwardly most striking was the modified nose with a radar dome to accommodate the RP-1 Izumrud-radar situated above the air intake, similar to that of the MiG-15Pbis. Other changes for the SP-7 were altered armament and a longer fuselage. As the need for radar-equipped fighters was very pressing at the time, work proceeded on several aircraft simultaneously at a brisk tempo. Finally about 100 MiG-17P's ("Fresco-B") were delivered to the Soviet Air Force and another 20 to the Air Defence Command. This MiG-17 version was the first Soviet light radar-equipped jet interceptor. The MiG-17LL "flying laboratory" saw service to test extendible leading-edge slats.

In the summer of 1952 based on the MiG-17P, the MiG-17PF appeared under project designation SP-7F. The difference from the previous type was in modifications and a Sirena-2 radar-warning receiver. On the other hand the MiG-17RF was a fighter-reconnaissance aircraft with cameras in the fuselage nose or in wing pods. Licensed reproductions of the PF appeared in Czechoslovakia as S-14 and as J-5A (J-5 Jia) in China.

At the end of 1953 in the MiG-17PFU (SP-6) there appeared a MiG-17PF with a modified radar and steering console for two radar-guided air-to-air guided missiles K-5 (NATO code "Alkali"). The same number of non-guided rockets as the "Alklai" could also be carried.The number of cannons aboard the prototype SP-6

The MiG-17 was a legend for friend and foe, as was its predecessor, the MiG-15 (Georg Mader).

The MiG-17 was the logical, increased-performance successor to the MiG-15 and was also a great export success. (Georg Mader)

was reduced to make way for the rockets, and with the MiG-17PFU series were disposed of altogether. The overall performance of the PFU fell somewhat below that of the MiG-17PF, but from 1957 a total of 56 MiG-17PF's were taken out of frontline service and returned to the manufacturer to be given the standard of the PFU. Upon their appearance at the frontline units in 1957 these variants were the first fighters in Europe to be equipped exclusively

The MiG-17SDK-5 was used to try out the guidance system for the air-to-ground K-10 guided weapon. (Butkiewicz)

with air-to-air guided weapons. A completion batch of the MiG-17 PFU was delivered to Air Defence Command PVO, receiving from the West the code-name "Fresco-E". During the production of the MiG-17 some machines were extracted from the series run and used as test vehicles for various projects. Project SN, which first flew in mid-1953, differed most greatly from the series versions. As with MiG-15 project SU, machine cannons were mounted in the nose of the fuselage which the pilot could operate remotely over a field of fire. In contrast to the SU, the fuselage of the SN was lengthened from cross-frame 13 forward by 1.07 metres and the nose closed so that air for the engine plant passed through two inlets at the wing roots alongside the cockpit.

Mounted immediately behind the aircraft nose on the left side were two 23mm TKB 495 machine cannons and a third on the right side at the same level. These could all be fired by the pilot using electrical remote control and traversed from -9° to +27°. A total of 15,000 rounds could be fired from a fixed ammunition chamber by this SV-25 weapons system. Because of the increased weight and greater fuel requirement, linked to decreased range, project SN was not proceeded with. Other MiG-17 prototypes were used for various rocketry experiments. These were SI-05, SI-07, SI-16, SI-19, SI-21, SI-21m, SI-91, SP-9 and SP-11. On SP-8 a radar visor of the "Grand" type was tried and on the SP-10 – originally a MiG-17PF – an experimental twin-barrelled 23mm machine-cannon installed. The MiG-17 with series number 214 was given modified wings as SI-10 and used from December 1954 for research into greater manoevrability. As a replacement for the "flying laboratory" MiG-9, the armament was removed from the seventh

The Polish LiM-6bis was a ground-attack version of the MiG-17 completed under licence.

The Chinese firm Shenjang, which also built the MiG-17 under licence, was the only manufacturer to offer a two-seater version of this type. The photo shows a Pakistani FT-5 in 1991.

MiG-17 prototype and the machine designated SDK-5.

In 1951 SDK-5 was given a guidance system for the air-to-ground K-10 guided weapon (NATO-Code AS-2 "Kipper") with aerials in the nose and at the stern.

On 3 August 1951 the Soviet Air Force ordered from OKB MiG a reconnaissance version MiG-17R with a Klimov VK-5F turbojet of 3,000 kgs thrust. The reconnaissance prototype SR-2 was fitted with an AFA-BA-21 camera and first flew in June 1952, and although this did not lead to a special photo-reconnaissance version of the MiG-17, the AFA-BA-21 camera and MAG-9 recorder was installed aboard a long line of series-type MiG-17F's of the Soviet Air Force.

On 21 April 1951 OKB MiG received approval for an MiGbis-45° prototype with two Mikulin AM-5A jet engines each of 2000 kgs thrust. Testing of this aircraft began in December under the name SM-1, the NII giving it the designation I-340. It was the first Mikoyan-Gurevitch machine to have a parachute canopy for braking, previously only the Polish licence versions LiM-5 and LiM-6 had been so equipped. Soon after flight testing began, the two AM-5A turbojets were exchanged for the more efficient Mikulin AM-5F's. With these the SM-1 showed convincing speed and climb performance.

I-350

OKB 155 (MiG) had occupied itself with studies for a supersonic fighter, and on 10 June 1950 the Kremlin approved the development of an experimental aircraft designated I-350, project M. The prototype would receive a Lyulka TR 3-A turbojet of 4,600 kgs thrust without afterburner, this having the great advantage of being available that same year. A completely new wing profile was designed for this supersonic fighter, and compared to the MiG-17 SI prototypes under test that year, the fuselage was distinctly longer and the control surfaces larger. All steering controls were activated hydraulically and an RP-1 Izumrud radar installed at the nose. The undercarriage had minor changes from the MiG-17. The I-350 underwent its maiden flight on 16 June 1951. This lasted only nine minutes due to technical problems. During the landing approach the engine stopped suddenly causing the hydraulic steering system to fail. The pilot succeeded in keeping the aircraft under control and dropped the wheels by means of bottled compressed air

Aircraft type:	I-350
Purpose:	Fighter prototype
Crew:	1
Engine plant:	1 x Lyulka TR-3A-turbojet, 4600 kgs thrust
Wingspan:	9.73 m, length 16.65 m
Wing area:	36 sq.m
Weight empty:	6125 kgs
Max take-off weight:	8710 kgs
Top speed:	(low level) 1240 kms/hr (10000 m) 1266 kms/hr
Ceiling:	16,600 m
Rate of climb to 5,000m:	1 min 6 secs 10,000m, 2 mins 36 secs
Range:	1620 kms (with supplementary tank). Armament 1 x 37mm N37 MK, 2 x 23mm N-23 MK

carried especially for such emergencies. Five more short test flights followed this incident over the next few weeks. After that, project M was abandoned because the TR-3A turbine was not yet ready for operational service. Further versions were planned but never built, these were the I-350M-2 with Korshun radar and the I-350MT, a two-seater trainer.

The I-350 was a project for a supersonic fighter with RP-1 Izumrud radar (Butkiewicz).

As the Lyulka TR-3A engine for the I-350 was not yet operational, the project was abandoned and two further planned prototypes not proceeded with (Butkiewicz).

-360

After the experience with the experimental M-1, OKB MiG was contracted to develop another prototype with two turbojets. This was the former SI-2 now known as the SM-2, and given the designation I-360/1 by NII, the Scientific Research Institute. From July 1951 the development of SM-2 had great priority. An aircraft was aimed for of smaller dimensions but with better performance than the single-jet I-350 had shown. Propulsion was supplied by two Mikulin AM-5A turbojets. After wind tunnel experiments at TsAGI, the Central Institute for Aero- and Hydro-Dynamics, the elevators were raised from the rear of the fuselage to just under the top edge of the rudder. Two N-37D machine cannons were installed in the wingroots. Towards the middle of May 1952 all conversion work was completed and the I-360-01 made its maiden flight on 24 May. It was soon obvious that the SM-2 would not pass through the sound barrier with the 2 x 2000 kgs thrust from the AM-5A jets and therefore

Aircraft type:	SM-9/1
Purpose:	Fighter-prototype
Crew:	1
Engine plant:	2 x Mikulin AM-9B (Tumanski RD-9B) turbojets, 3,250 kgs thrust
Wingspan:	9 m, length 14.08 m
Wing area:	25.16 sq.m
Weight empty:	about 5090 kgs
Max take-off weight:	7360 kgs
Top speed:	(low level) 1150 kms/hr (10,000 m) 1451 kms/hr
Ceiling:	17,500 m
Armament:	3 x 23mm NR-23 MK, 120 rounds each. Drop-payload up to 1 tonne

these were replaced at the end of 1952 by two Mikulin AM-5F turbines providing 2150 kgs thrust each. On the next test flight a series of technical problems came to light which had to be overcome at once. During this work the fuselage was given steel sheeting near the muzzles of the two cannon in the wingroots to protect against flash. As the result of further

The I-360/1 was an experimental aircraft with two Mikulin AM-9B turbines and had elevators higher on the rudder than the second prototype. (Butkiewicz)

The second prototype I-360/2 had two revised Tumanski RD-9B turbojets and was the forerunner for the MiG 19 (Butkiewicz).

tests the elevators of the machine, now known as SM-2A (I-360/2), were taken down from the rudder head and relocated at fuselage level.

After changes to the protective outer layers on the wing surfaces and elsewhere, the aircraft finally received the designation SM-2B. In the March 1953 test at NII the machine still failed to reach the set target speeds although four months later in a second test run a speed of 1,400 kms/hr was achieved in diving flight.

In 1954 when the Aleksandr Mikulin design bureau completed work on the new AM-9

turbojet under the direction of Sergei Tumanski one of these was fitted aboard SM-2B the following year. After Mikulin retired, Tumanski revised the engine which eventually entered production as RD-9B. The new engine and a modification to the armament led to a re-designation of the aircraft as SM-9/1, which took to the air for the first time on 5 January 1954. Many reports state that this aircraft set a world record with a climb performance of 180m/sec and prepared the way for the first Soviet supersonic fighter, the MiG-19.

The prototype I-360/2 was also designated SM-2A (Butkiewicz).

MiG-19

To complement the SM-9/1 undergoing testing, in January 1954 two further prototypes, SM-9/2 and SM-9/3 were ordered and completed. 9/2 first flew on 16 September 1954 and 9/3 on 27 November 1955. In the course of testing, accompanied by a series of modifications, both aircraft reached Mach 1.46 in diving flight and finally the series production of the MiG-19 ("Farmer A") and MiG-19F was begun.

On 28 August 1954 the SM-7/1 based on the SM-9 made its maiden flight, equipped with an Izumrud radar and doing service as a first prototype for the all-weather interceptor MiG-19P. In 1955 the second prototype SM-7/2 followed it and in the same year MiG-19P (ASCC code "Farmer B") went into series production mainly for delivery to the Soviet Air Force, PVO Air Defence Command and the FA (Aviation Front). The series production of the MiG-19S (S=stabiliser) began in 1955 and also of its offspring MiG-19SF, designated "Farmer C" in

the West, with oscillating control surfaces. The Poles named the licence-built MiG-19S as LiM-7 and the Czechs S-105. Later it was series built

Aircraft type:	MiG-19S
Purpose:	Fighter
Crew:	1
Engine plant:	2 x Mikulin AM-9B (Tumanski RD-9B) turbojets, 3250 kgs thrust each
Wingspan:	9 m, length 14.8m, wing area, 25.16 sq.m
Weight empty:	5172 kgs
Max take-off weight:	7560 kgs
Top speed:	(low level) 1100 kms/hr (10000 m) 1454 kms/hr
Ceiling:	17500 m
Rate of climb (5000 m):	24 secs, (15000 m) 2 mins 36 secs
Climb performance:	115 m/sec
Range:	1390/2200 kms (without/with outboard tanks)
Armament:	3 x 30mm NR-30 MK, up to 500 kg payload

The Chinese manufacturer Shenjang built various versions of the MiG-19 under licence, including for export, such as this F-6 for the Pakistani Air Force.

The Shenjang FT-6 was one of several two-seater trainer versions manufactured in China.

by Shenjang for the Chinese Air Force as the single-seat J-6 (MiG-19SF), J-6A (PF), J-6B (PM), J-6C (an improved J-6), J-6 Xin (new) and improved J-6A, as a bomber and reconnaissance version JZ-6, and also as the dual-seaters JJ-6, CJ-6, F-6 and FT-6.

In the course of the MiG-19 series production more than fifty machines, mainly MiG-19S, were held back by OKB MiG for experimental purposes. Amongst them were four MiG-19S of the series run tested as SMR prototypes with reconnaissance equipment from which a small series of MiG-19R reconnaissance aircraft with camera-bays evolved. At the same time six machines of the training version MiG-19UTI (UTI MiG-19) were developed with a tandem-cockpit but these never made series production. The MiG-19SW was an all-weather aircraft with heavier armament.

In 1955 the SM-21 was used for trials with a non-guided air-to-ground S-21 rocket and at the same time work began on the converted SM-9/1 prototype, now renumbered SM-30. SM-30M was a mock-up, but SM-30/1 and 30/2 were used for a series of oblique take-off experiments in which the aircraft were transported on a wheeled ramp which could be inclined 15° upwards. A PRD-22 rocket providing a thrust of up to 40 tonnes within 2.5 seconds was mounted below the fuselage to catapult the SM-30 into the skies, where its own engine cut in after three seconds. Because of the dangerous nature of these experiments the first three were carried out unmanned and the first hellfire ride for a pilot took place on 14 April 1957.

In August 1956 work started on a new version of the SM-9 intended to engage high altitude reconnaissance versions of the British Canberra and other high-flying targets then making repeated incursions into Soviet airspace. Another experimental prototype was the SM-9V with two Mikulin AM-9BF turbines for high altitude flight but neither cannons nor armour. In a test flight for NII the aircraft reached a height of 20,740 metres and Air Defence Command PVO ordered a small series of these interceptor fighters as MiG-19SV at the conclusion of trials.

In January 1956 orders went out for a version of the MiG-19 with four K-5 "Alkali" air-to-air

The SM-10 was used for mid-air refuelling trials from a Tupolev Tu-16N.

guided missiles, and from these the prototype SM-7/M resulted. This led to the all-weather interceptor MiG-19PF ("Farmer D"), soon followed by the MiG-19PM ("Farmer E") fitted with the new RP-2 Izumrud radar. The SM-7/M flew for the first time at the end of January 1956 and soon afterwards as MiG-19PM entered series production – mainly for the PVO. A second experimental machine designated SM-7/2M underwent tests as from 14 October 1957 and was used to try out the improved K-5M rocket. These results led at the beginning of 1958 to the series production of the MiG-19PMU. Other MiG-19's served that year as SM-10 for air-to-air refuelling trials with the

Tupolev Tu-16N "Badger", in which ten-hour missions with two refuelling operations were aimed for. With the SM-21 the radio-navigation systems Svod and Gorizont were tried out and the SM-52P – a former MiG-19P – was used to try out the Almaz (diamond) radar. From October 1956 the SM-20 was used in the development of a radio-control system for the Mikoyan-Gurevitch air-to-ground guided missile K-20 known in the West as AS-3 "Kangaroo" and carried operationally by a Tupolev Tu-95N "Bear".

At the beginning of 1957 the SM-12/1 was fitted with two Tumanski RD-9BF-2 turbojets providing a total of 7,695 kgs of thrust for a top speed of 1930 kms/hr. In mid-1957 the

The SM-12/1 was fitted with two Tumanski RD9BF-2 turbojets in 1957 (Butkiewicz).

The SM-12/3 was tried out with Mikulin R3-26 turbojets (Butkiewicz).

The fourth prototype was the SM-12PM which could carry four radar-guided air-to-air guided missiles (Butkiewicz).

Besides "Alkali" guided missiles the SM-12PMU was also used to test rocket motors (Butkiewicz).

The I-370 based on the MiG-19 had a Klimov VK-7 turbojet (Butkiewicz).

When work on the Klimov VK-3 turbojet was terminated, it also meant the end for the experimental carrier I-3 in August 1956 (Butkiewicz

SM-12/2 and SM-12/3 propelled by Mikulin R3-26 jets each giving 3500 kgs thrust and equipped with new control instruments made their appearance. At the end of that year the fourth prototype SM-12PM was completed, able to carry four radar-guided K-5M air-to-air missiles.

In order to investigate turbojet problems at high altitudes, in 1957 the prototype SM-20/P came into service and in 1957 and 1958 the SM-K/1 and SM-K/2 were used for the remote control of the supersonic K-22 air-to-ground guided missile (AS-4 "Kitchen").

At the beginning of 1958, trials were carried out on the SM-12PMU. This aircraft was fitted with two Mikulin R3M-26 turbojets each providing 3800 kgs of thrust and able to carry unguided missiles in pods and also the "Alkali" guided missile. The SM-50 (MiG-19SU) and its further developments SM-51 and SM-52 were used for experiments with rocket motors. The SM-9/3, which made its second maiden flight on 11 February 1959 as the conversion SM-9/3T, was part of the test programme for the new K-13 air-to-air guided missile (AA-2 "Atoll") and was joined a few months later by the SM-6 The SM-6 was also used to test the K-6 air-to-air guided missile, but this did not enter series production. In 1975 details were received in the West for the first time about a version of the Shenjang F-6 built in China and known initially as the Nanshang Quiang-5 (Q-5). This model

An SM-20 being released from a Tupolev Tu-95 "Bear".

Some SM-30 experimental units were launched up a trailer ramp.

had a completely redesigned forward area, the central air intake being replaced by two apertures either side of the cockpit. The export version of the Q-5 given the ASCC code "Fantan" was designated A-5.

OKB MiG also designed a series of progressive prototypes based on the MiG-19. Thus in May 1953 the I-370 prototype, known at the works as I-1, was built housing a Klimov VK-7 turbojet providing 6270 kgs of thrust. The I-2 with a less swept wing, also based on the I-350, failed to meet specifications and was abandoned. The successor I-380, also known as I-3, was expected by the Soviet leadership to be the new first line fighter. The Klimov VK-3 turbojet with afterburner was expected to provide 8440 kgs of thrust, but this was given up in 1956 and also meant the end for the I-3. In parallel to this was an all-weather interceptor project, the I-3P, fitted with an Almaz radar system, also shelved at the end of 1954. The I-3U followed the two I-3 prototypes fitted with the Uragan-1 weapons control system, VK-3 turbojet and Almaz radar.

This aircraft was also designated I-5, I-410 by NII, and was completed in 1956 but never flew – as previously mentioned – after work on the Klimov VK-3 turbine was halted.

The Nanchang Q-5 was an extreme conversion of a MiG-19 to a fighter-bomber, delivered to Pakistan here as A-5C.

Various rocket motors were tried out with the SM-50.

When the I-7U was seriously damaged in June 1956, it returned to GAZ-155 works for conversion into the I-75 (Butkiewicz).

The E.150 appeared in December 1955 in response to demands for an interceptor able to engage the supersonic Convair B-58 "Hustler" and the high altitude Lockheed U-2 reconnaissance machine. (Butkiewicz).

After the end of project I-3 in August 1956 the Soviet Air Force asked OKB for more development work on an all-weather interceptor with a different engine plant. The I-7 (I-7U) appeared, based on the I-3U, equipped with two Lyulka AL-7 turbojets and carrying two NR-23 cannon at four positions on the wings and also various rockets and guided missiles.

Maiden flight was on 22 April 1957. When a wing of the I-7U was damaged while landing on 21 June of the same year, the project was abandoned after seven test flights and the prototype went to GAZ 155 for conversion into the I-75F or I-7K. On 7 March 1957 OKB MiG received the order to design a high-altitude aircraft without armament. Almost exactly one year later the prototype I-75 flew for the first time at LII Flight Research Institute with a Lyulka AI-7F turbojet: the new Uragan-5 weapons control system was not installed until 28 April 1958. That same year the second prototype I-75F, the converted former I-7U, took to the air, but both prototypes were given up on 11 May 1959 when the Soviet Air Force chose the competitor's Suchoi Su-9 as its new interceptor.

In the second half of the 1950s the Soviet air fleet had an urgent need for a fast high altitude interceptor able to engage the supersonic Convair B-58 bomber "Hustler" and the Lockheed U-2 spy plane flying at 27,000 metres. Thus the prototype E-150 came into being, incorporating what had been learned from its predecessors I-75 and E-4. Armament

The I-3 served from the end of 1956 under designation I-3U as a carrier for the new weapons control system Urugan-2.

In the summer of 1956 the Soviet Air Force required another all-weather interceptor to replace the abandoned I-3, and as a result the I-7U was developed.

was the MiG-developed, almost 4.5-metres long air-to-air K-9 guided weapon known to the West as the AA-4 "Awl". Although the E-150 was ready in December 1958, the first flight was delayed until 8 July 1960 due to problems developing the Tumanski R-15-300 turbojet. This eighteen month pause in development naturally meant the end of the project, but before it was cancelled by OKB MiG on 26 January 1962, the E-150 had flown 42 test flights with three different jet engines.

MiG-21

Benefiting from the experience gained in the Korean War, in the autumn of 1953 work began on a new lightweight fighter able to reach Mach 2 at 20,000 metres. Similar efforts in the United States led to the Lockheed F-104A "Starfighter". The first plans at OKB MiG produced in January 1954 the studies E-1 and X-1 with reduced wing areas, initially designed for a Mikulin AM-5A, but later fitted with an AM-9B jet engine. The prototype was redesignated E-2 and X-2 for the change of turbojets. With the AM-9B the E-2 reached Mach 1.8. Two experimental machines E-4 were then built with differing Delta wing surfaces. The best engine choice for this new aircraft proved to be the Mikulin AM-11 ready for service in 1955, fitted to the first of the two E-4's for the maiden flight. MiG's GAZ 155 built subsequently four more prototypes to try out the two Delta-wing versions – two machines each for every wing variation. The first of these additions was the E-5 (X-5 at NII) which had

Aircraft type:	MiG-21F-13
Purpose:	Fighter
Crew:	1
Engine plant:	1 x Tumanski R-11F-330 je 5740 kgs thrust
Wingspan:	7.15m, length 15.76 m
Wing area:	23 sq.m
Weight empty:	4871 kgs
Max take-off weight:	8625 kgs
Top speed:	(low level) 1100 kms/hr (12,500 m) 2175 kms/hr
Ceiling:	19,000 m
Rate of climb to 19,000 m:	13 mins 30 secs
Range:	1670 kms (with outboard tank)
Armament:	1 x 30mm NR-30 MK, 2 x K-13 guided missiles plus 1490 kgs payload

been originally labelled E-4/2 and first flew on 9 January 1956. The type designation MiG-21 was proposed for the serial run of machines arising from these prototypes. However the ne' Mikulin AM-9B turbine, which had been

The E-2 was the second prototype in a project in which the attempt was made in 1953 to create a fighter which could reach Mach 2 at 20,000 metres.

The MiG-21F was the first version of this type delivered to the North Vietnamese aerial forces.

modified during the year by Sergei Tumanski and renamed R-11, was still not ready to enter service and the engine caught fire on the ground on 20 January. After repair eight more test flights ensued until the turbine broke down again on 19 May at which the testing of the first E-5 was terminated on 18 October 1956 and the aircraft returned to GAZ-155. Before this on 22 March one of the two E-2A machines with swept wings had flown. Five pre-series aircraft were built to the E-2A design, receiving the designation MiG-23 and the ASCC code "Faceplate", and with the AM-11 (R-11) jet engine reached Mach 1.79.

In the quest for increased performance and the ideal jet engine, in 1954 OKB MiG decided on a mixture of propulsive methods, a turbojet plus a fixed rocket motor built into the E-50 (U-2) prototype. There were three of these, based on the E-2A and designated E-50/1, E-50/2 and E-50/3. The E-50/1 made its maiden flight on the same day as the E-5, and the rocket unit was used for the first time on 8 June 1956.

Because the first prototype had been damaged while landing, shortly afterwards the E-50/2 made test flights in which on 17 June 1957 an altitude of 25,600 metres was attained and a top speed of 2,460 kms/hr achieved.

Two machines designated E-4 were built with varying Delta wings.

The E-5 was a further prototype on the road to the MiG-21 and flew for the first time in January 1956.

During further trials the E50/2 rocket motor caught fire, destroying the aircraft. However the test results led to the E-50A, equipped with a Tumanski R-11 turbine above a Dushkin S-155 rocket motor, twenty of the latter having been built for localised air defence machines. The design bureau of L. S. Dushkin was closed at this time and no series production of the E-50A ensued.

In December 1956 OKB MiG decided to retain the Delta configuration for its next fighter and while GAZ-21 prepared the series production of the MiG-21 Mikoyan's GAZ-155 began work on the pre-series E-6/1, E-6/2 and E-6/3, but before the maiden flight of E-6/3 the preparations for the series run of the first series version MiG-21F (E-6T) had been concluded. In December 1958 E-6T was flown at NII and in the

Two prototypes of the E-8 were built which had air intakes beneath the cabin.

The E50/2 had swept wings and a rocket motor in tandem with a turbojet.

In 1966 an Iraki pilot flew this MiG-21F to Israel. After extensive investigation the machine is now an exhibition at the Israeli Aviation Museum, Hatzerim.

The MiG-21PF fitted with a Safir radar evolved from the E-7 prototype.

year following the first MiG-21's were delivered. The third pre-series machine now re-designated E-6T/3 (E-6T-K-13) was tested as the carrier for the air-to-air guided missile K-13 (R3S and AA-2 "Atoll-A") and the E-6T-DS was an experimental aircraft with leading edge slats. All pre-series machines were given the name "Fishbed-B" in the West. The MiG-21F's delivered to India were designated by them Type 74.

Because the MiG-21F was the simplest version of this new fighter, the first of two experimental models E-7, which had improved electronics besides other modifications, flew on 10 August 1958 leading to the series version MiG-21P of June 1960. The testing of the two E-7's also resulted in the MiG-21PF being fitted with the new Safir radar. In the experimental E-76, a modified PF, some "world records for women" were achieved. The subsequent MiG-21FL was a simplified PF export version for completion under licence at Hindustan Aeronautics Ltd in India. The MiG-21PF was also turned out in China as the Xian J-2. The

MiG-21PFV on the other hand was the Type 77 export version for Viet Nam. The MiG-21PF and the FL were known in the West as "Fishbed-D" after being incorrectly designated MiG-22 for a short while and tagged MiG-22PFF in the United States. Variants of the PF were the MiG-21PFS also known as MiG-21PF (SPS) with blown flaps, the MiG-21PF-13, MiG-21-17, MiG-21PF-31 all known as "Fishbed-E". Other prototypes for export versions were the E-074, the E-77 and the E-88.

On 28 April 1961 the E-66A, converted from the E-6T/1 and fitted with a packet of Dushkin S3/20 booster rockets, broke the world altitude record with a direct ascent to 34,714 metres. On 9 July 1961, the second prototype of the E-6V used to experiment short take-offs, flew at Tushino. Two SU-1500 rocket motors were mounted under the elevators for this purpose providing the E6V/2 with supplementary thrust of 3,500 kgs for ten seconds. Later the machine was also used to test a wheels/ski chassis combination.

The Hungarian MiG-21PF still wore the red star as the national marking in 1990.

By the following year 1991, Hungary's military aircraft – in the photo another MiG-21PF – wore the tricolour-chevron from the pre-Communist era.

The Slovak air force also wore its own national markings after the break up of Czechoslovakia – in the photo a MiG-21MF just taking off.

A MiG-21MF at Caslav, Czech Republic, in 2004 (Georg Mader).

The MiG-21PD was a variant with a lift engine in the fuselage to improve short take-off characteristics (Butkiewicz).

During their civil war, a Yugoslav pilot defected to Klagenfurt in Austria on 25 October 1991 with this MiG-21MF. The tactical markings of the aircraft have already been painted over here. The machine is today the property of the Army Historical Museum in Vienna (Guido Hitzenhammer).

In 1961 two experimental interceptor-fighters designations E-8/1 and E-8/2, also known as MiG-23 at NII, appeared whose most notable outward variation from other MiG-21 versions was an air intake under the cockpit. Flight testing of both aircraft took place in 1962 and ended with an engine failure in which the E-8/1 pilot was hurt.

On 17 October 1960 the dual-seater training version MiG-21U (MiG-21UTI, E-6U) based on the MiG-21F-13 and given the ASCC codename "Mongol-A" made its maiden flight. In 1965 the Indian Air Force ordered some of these two-seaters, calling them Type 66-400. Chinese productions of this

trainer under licence were known as Chengdu FT-7 while the Rumanian Air Force armed its MiG-21U's calling them "Lancer-B's". In 1965 a Soviet female pilot flew a dual-seater E-33 to 24,336 metres to a "world record altitude for women".

The MiG-21F-13 was delivered to the squadrons as from 15 January 1963 and equipped with the K-13 guided missile as standard, but it could also carry various types of rocket pod. The type was replicated in India, in Czechoslovakia as S-106 and at Shenjang in China as J-7, later Xian F-7. The MiG-21F and its licensed reproductions were designated "Fishbed-C" in the West.

In 1963 trials were made using the experimental E-7SPS with blown flaps to improve manouevrability at low speeds. The results of these tests were integrated into the development of the MiG-21PFM, fitted with the newest electronics and, as an alternative to the "Atoll", also received RS-2US ("Alkali") air-to-air rockets.

In East Germany this version MiG-21SPS was

This Angolan MiG 21MF without wings was photographed in South Africa in 1992.

85 ∎

A MiG-21bis of the Croatian Air Force taking off from Pula in 2005 (Georg Mader).

fitted with a cannon mount GP-9 and designated MiG-21 SPS-K. On 16 June 1966 the MiG-21PD (E-7PD), a converted PFM fitted with a lift engine in the centre of the fuselage to help shorten the take-off run, made its maiden flight, but after flight testing the MiG-21PD was cancelled the following year. Although the modifications to the MiG-21PD provided no advantages worth mentioning over its contemporaries, some of these variants were built, known in the West as "Fishbed-G". One of these was aircraft 21-14, tested as an unmanned attack aircraft. In the MiG-21PFS delivered to only one Soviet aviation regiment the pilot could select one of two performance levels for the afterburner. All MiG-21PF and PFM variants were designated "Fishbed-F" in the West.

The MiG-21R was a spy-plane fitted with systems for day- and night-photography and also infra-red and ELINT (electronic intelligence) reconnaissance. This version was given the codename "Fishbed-H" by ASCC. Besides other modifications the MiG-21S (E-7S) had a total of

After the end of the civil war, Croatia now operated former Yugoslav MiG-21bis.

Two MiG-21/I1 "Analog" were used to research wing-forms for the supersonic airliner Tupolev Tu-144 "Charger".

The second trainer version based on the MiG-21MF was the MiG-21UM. (Georg Mader)

This is a Finnish MiG-21UM.

The armed Mig-21U's of the Rumanian Air Force were designated "Lancer-B".

five pylons and as the first Soviet MiG-21 variant could carry a GP-9 cannon and tactical nuclear weapons at the inner wing positions. The MiG-21SM had a GSh-23L machine cannon in the fuselage at the expense of less fuel. Another variant was the MiG-21SMB. The MiG-21M was a simplified export version of the MiG-212SM, and together with the MiG-21PFMA (MiG-21MA), whose prototype was designated E-9, was known in the West as "Fishbed J". This was given the classification Type 88 by the Indian Air Force. The MiG-21MF, a MiG-21M with the turbojet and radar of the SM, also received the ASCC code "Fishbed-J". The MiG-21RF, a reconnaissance aircraft, and the MiG-21MT which came next with greater fuel capacity were both tagged "Fishbed-K", as was the MiG-21SMT, based on the MT version but with

After the year 2000 the Rumanians reckoned on good prospects of sales of their "Lancer-B" to the West.

The Czech military aircraft test centre VZLU used these MiG-21UM's for ejector-seat trials.

A Hungarian MiG-21UM and a MiG-21PF at the Taszar air force base near Lake Balaton in 1992.

Towards the end of the 1980s Chinese Xian FT-7's were often guests at Western air shows.

improved fuel and electronic systems. Based on Vietnam War experience, OKB MiG developed the MiG-21bis (E-7bis) as a low-level jet fighter, series production of which began in 1972. Sub-variants were the MiG-21bis-SAU (with SAU-21 autopilot), MiG-21bisLazur (with Lazur electronics) and MiG-21bisN (as a carrier for tactical nuclear weapons). These MiG-21bis variants were designated "Fishbed-L" and "Fishbed-N" in the West. Within the framework of the development of the supersonic airliner Tupolev Tu-144 "Charger", two MiG-21S of the series production were redesignated MiG-21I and "Analog", also A-144, and converted to a slightly modified wing form similar to that envisaged for the Tu-144. The MiG-21I1 made its maiden flight on 18 April 1968 but crashed a year later. The second prototype MiG-21I/2 flew in the same year and at the completion of trials was exhibited at the Moscow Air Force Museum.

The MiG-21E was a remote-controlled subsonic version of the MiG-21PF and PFM developed jointly with the Kazan Aviation Institute. Up to the year 1969 a number of MiG-21E's were converted at various Soviet Air Force workshops. As a further development of the MiG-21U dual seater, the MiG-21US, based on the MiG-21MF, appeared, replicated at HAL in India as Type 66-600. In June 1974 one of these machines, designated E-33 again, created a new world altitude record for women which was exceeded five months later by an E-66B. These new training variants, and the last two-

seater variant MiG-21UM, received in the West the code "Mongol-B".

The MiG-21-93 was the last version of this jet fighter. It was a completely renovated MiG-21 with new radar and introduced to the public at the Farnborough Air Show in 1994 and at the Berlin ILA. At about the same time in the mid-1990's the newest Chinese version of the MiG-21, Xian F-7M "Airguard" was introduced, resulting from project "Super 7", equipped with a new engine and western electronics, and also the FT-7 dual seater version.

This Xian F-7 belongs to the Zimbabwean Air Force.

Pakistan was also a repeat client for the Chinese aviation industry – in the photo Xian F-7P.

This MiG-21PF with East German markings is shown here on a visit to Twenthe in Holland – most probably after the political change. (Peter P. K .Herrendorf)

This until now final version MiG-21-93 was exhibited at a number of air shows in Europe in 1994.

Heavy Fighters

In the second half of the 1950's, OKB MiG focussed on the need for a "heavy fighter" and began working on plans for two E-151 prototypes whose specialities were to be two traversable TKB 495 machine-cannons in the nose and behind the cockpit. This project was never realized and remained a "paper tiger"

although it did lead to the development of a smaller air intake installed on the successor E-152. The plans for the prototype were complete even before the high altitude interceptor E-150 and now it was aimed for a speed of Mach 3 with a Tumanski R-15 turbojet. Because of the increasing delays in series-producing the R-15, which meant the end of the E-150, the E-152 was modified to take two Tumanski R-11F-300 turbojets – available singly in the MiG-21F-13 –

The E-152-2 became the E-152M, a fighter with a large range.

and redesignated E-152A. The first prototype flew on 10 July 1959 and had made 55 flights by 6 August 1960. In the following year the E-152A was shown to the public for the first time at Tushino and subsequently served as the experimental carrier for various guided missiles until the fatal crash in 1965 which destroyed the aircraft and killed its pilot. The West incorrectly identified the E-152A as the MiG-23 and awarded it the codename "Flipper". When the

Because the R-15 turbojet was not yet operational, two Tumanski R-11F-300 were installed in the prototype which was then redesignated E-152-A.

The E-152-1 broke a world speed record in June 1962 and was redesignated E-166.

As a heavy fighter, the E-152 was fitted with a Tumanski R-15-turbojet to achieve Mach 3. (Butkiewicz).

Tumanski R-15-300 turbojet was finally availabl from mid-1960, it was fitted aboard the E-152-1 which was basically an E-152A, differing from it outwardly by its engine and larger wings. An Urugan-5-B radar was built into the non-adjustable cone of the air intake, while other refinements were also made. The E-152-1 made its maiden flight on 21 April 1961 at LII Flight Research Institute and on the following 7 October created a new world record by flying a 100-km circular course at 2,401 kms/hr. The next world record of this kind ensued on 7 June 1962 at 2,681 kms/hr, the aircraft on both

occasions being officially described as E-166. On 21 September 1961 at the Shukovski Air Force Academy, flight testing began of the E-152-2, a model differing only in minor details from the E-152-1, and a short time later the E-152-2 attained a speed of 2,740 kms/hr at an altitude of 22,500 metres. Inherent problems with the turbojet prevented further testing and the prototype was returned to the manufacturer. Because of the emphasis on further developing the air-to-air guided missile K-9 the test programme for the E-152-1 was broken off and not resumed until later, often with empty rocket rails. Evolving as a conversion from the returned E-152-2, the E-152M flew for the first time in the summer of 1961: this was to operate as an interceptor fighter with great range, equipped with the replaced K-80 or R4 (AA-5 "Ash") air-to air guided missiles. The original plans for project 152P included scaled- up leading-edge slats for the E-152M as were used on the E-152M. Because of aerodynamic and structural problems the E-152M made its maiden flight without them. The project was abandoned two years later in favour of the much more promising E-155.

MiG-25

In the first half of the 1960's when in the United States the nuclear bomber B-70 "Valkyrie" and the Lockheed A-12 fighter appeared, which could both reach Mach 3 and a ceiling of 24,000 metres, the urgent need grew in the Soviet Union for a suitable interceptor fighter in order to confront this new threat from the West as soon as possible. Based on projects E-150 and E-152, both of which had exceeded Mach 2, OKB MiG began work in cooperation with TsAGI on the development of the E-155 which could fly at 3,000 kms/hr. In the development of this new superlative interceptor the designers strayed from the former MiG-aircraft philosophy and the aircraft designated MiG-25 (prototype E-26) received two turbojets drawing air through two lateral intakes, a further innovation being a dual rudder system. In 1962 the decision was taken to adopt an interceptor designated MiG-25P and a reconnaissance version, MiG-25R. The reconnaissance prototype E-155R-1 first flew on 6 March 1964, the fighter prototype E-155P-1 on 9 September 1964. Three experimental versions of the fighter were built and seven of the spy plane. During testing of these ten prototypes, the E-155R-1, the E-155R-3 and the E-155P1 broke a number of speed, altitude and rate of climb records. Those machines aiming for these records between 1965 and 1973 were all designated E-266 and their more advanced successor continuing these records from 1975 to 1977 received from the Fédération Aéronautique Internationale (FAI) the designation E-266M.

The MiG-25 interceptor designated by the West "Foxbat-A" was operational with PVO in

Aircraft type:	MiG-25P
Purpose:	Interceptor
Crew:	1
Engine plant:	2 x Tumanski R-31 jet engines, 12,250 kp thrust
Wingspan:	13.95 m, length 23.82 m, height 6.1 m, wing area 56.83 sq.m
Weight empty:	20 tonnes*
Max take-off weight:	36.2 tonnes*
Top speed:	2975 kms/hr*
Ceiling:	24.4 kms*
Rate of climb (19,000 m):	13 mins 30 secs
Radius of action:	1450 kms*
Armament:	Up to four air-to-air guided missiles
*estimated	

1973 and was also exported to the Near East. From 1978 the series production of the MiG-25P was transferred to the MiG-25PD with a longer nose. Between 1979 and 1984 about 370 MiG-25P's were brought up to the standard of the MiG-25PD and after the conversion labelled 25PDS (MiG-25M) at which the West decided to call all MiG-25PD and PDS "Foxbat-E". A MiG-25PD was converted into a "flying laboratory" as aircraft 20-84. Series production of the reconnaissance variant MiG-25R ("Foxbat B") with cameras in the fuselage nose began in February 1969 although less than ten had been completed by the end of that year. After that from 1970 series production was given over to the next variant MiG-25RB which carried a larger bomb payload and received other modifications. MiG-25RB was delivered to other Warsaw Pact countries, the Near and Far East. In 1971 Soviet Air Force personnel accompanied aircraft bought by Egypt. A sub-variant of the MiG-25R was the MiG-25RBK, developed in parallel, which was intended for electronic

The E-155P-1, the prototype of the fighter variants, made its maiden flight in September 1965 (Georg Mader).

e dual-seater MiG-25U of 1968 was followed four years later by this MiG-25RU variant.

A Soviet Air Force MiG-25U prepares to land somewhere in East Germany at the end of the 1980's (Ing.Karl Brandel).

MiG-25RBSh and MiG-25RBF. All these electronic spy planes were designated "Foxba D" by NATO.

In 1968 the dual seat trainer/interceptor MiG-25U/MiG-25PU respectively took to the skies for the first time and four years later so their successor MiG-25RU. A MiG-25PU designated E-133 made new "world records fc women" between 1975 and 1978. All MiG-25RU's, of which some were used for testing the new ejector-seats and were nicknamed "Kresla" (armchair), and the MiG-25PU, were designated "Foxbat-C" in the West. The 22nd series machine of the MiG-25PU breed was converted into the "flying laboratory" MiG-25SOTN which monitored the landings of the space ferry BTS-002 of the Buran programme. Based on the MiG-25PB a further fighter versi appeared from 1972 with increased electronic equipment: this was designated "Foxbat-F" by the West.

reconnaissance as well as for use in fighter-bomber operations.

The MiG-25RBS was principally specialised for ELINT (electronic intelligence) work and from 1978 was replaced by the MiG-25RBV and MiG-25RBT variants which had better navigation systems. Further versions from 1981 were the

This single-seat MiG-25 was photographed in 1991 at Finow-Eberswalde.

MiG-23 and MiG-27

At the end of the 1960's OKB MiG began work on a fighter to combine a top speed higher than Mach 2 with STOL (short take-off and landing) ability in order to operate from small airfields unknown to NATO. The aircraft they had in mind was developed in two variants: the first prototype E-23 (E-230) had a delta-wing configuration similar to that of the MiG-21 and the second, designated E-231 (MiG-231) was a swing-wing fighter. STOL was achieved on the two MiG-23DPD prototypes 23-01 (MiG-23PD) and 23-11 (MiG-231G) by a Katchaturov R-27 lift engine in the centre of the fuselage. It was

Aircraft type:	MiG-23ML
Purpose:	Fighter
Crew:	1
Engine plant:	1 x Tumanski R-35-300 jet engine with max 127.53 kN thrust
Wingspan:	13.96 m (swung outwards) 7.78 m (swung inwards)
Length:	16.63 m, height 4.82 m, wing area 37.35 sq.m
Weight empty:	8472 kgs
Max take-off weight:	14,800 kgs
Top speed (11,000 m):	2500 kms/hr
Ceiling:	18500 m
Rate of climb:	152 m/sec
Radius of action:	700 kms
Armament:	1 x 23mm GSh-twin MK, 200 rounds, up to 2 tonnes payload

The E-231 was one of the two MiG-23 swing-wing prototypes. (Georg Mader)

The two MiG-23DPD had an additional lift engine in the fuselage.

not the intention to achieve a vertical take-off. The unarmed prototype 23-11 flew for the first time on 3 April 1967, the 23-01 on 9 July. Both machines were given the ASCC-code "Faithless". So many problems on the 23-11 swing-wings came to light during testing that an OKB MiG team was put together to resolve them. After a series of modifications mainly to do with flight stability, on its fourteenth test flight on 10 Jun 1967, the wings of the machine now designated 23-11/1 were swung repeatedly ar impressively. Testing was finished on 9 July 1968. Meanwhile another two prototypes without the additional lift engine had been built and received from the West the name "Flogger". As a quick intermediate solution, fo

At the end of the 1980's the Libyan Air Force had
four MiG-25U's for pilot training.

The additional lift engine in the fuselage was intended to improve the short take-off characteristics of the MiG-DPD and not to give it vertical take-off capability.

At the end of the 1980's the MiG-23MF's were the most modern bomber aircraft in the Hungarian Air Force.

MiG-23U, Finow-Eberswalde, 1991.

operational use on 28 May 1969 a MiG-23S of the pre-series flew, this machine being based on the mainframe of the 23/11/1 with a Safir 23 radar in its shorter nose and other modifications. The single-seater was also thought of for conversion training purposes. The production of the MiG-23S version was terminated at the end of 1970 after about fifty machines had been built. Subsequently the MiG-23SM made its appearance, being a MiG-23S with four wing pylons. In the West this was lumped together with its predecessors and designated "Flogger-A". Parallel to the MiG-23S, from the end of 1967 OKB MiG developed tandem-seat training versions of this swing-wing aircraft known as MiG-23U, MiG-23UB and

Tucked away amongst fields of maize in the Hungarian Air Force base where MiG-23MF and Suchoi Su-20 "Fitter" were stationed.

A Hungarian MiG-23MF on a visit to Bratislava, 1992.

MiG-23UM. Two prototypes flew for the first time in May 1969, the series production of the type known in the West as "Flogger-C" ran from 1970 until 1978. In June 1972 the single seater MiG-23M flew as the first of the series version, differing from the MiG-23S with a number of improvements. After that came the export version MiG-23MS with simplified electronics. Another export version was the MiG-23MF, which together with the MiG-23M and MS was tagged "Flogger-B" in the West. "Flogger-E" was a variant of the MiG-23MF with remodelled forward fuselage and simplified equipment. A more advanced interceptor of the MiG-23MF was the MiG-23ML with a maximum all-up weight 3,700 kgs lighter than that of its predecessors. The ML proved a sales hit and received the ASCC code "Flogger-G". A sub-version of the ML was the MLA with different weight carrying possibilities and the MiG-23P with broader electronics for pursuits developed specially for PVO Air Defence Command, also classified in the West as "Flogger-G". From 1981 all Soviet Air Force MiG-23ML were upgraded to the newest technical level in the framework of technical inspections and redesignated MiG-23MLD, NATO considering them now to be "Flogger-K".

In 1969 OKB MiG began its first studies for a new ground-attack aircraft designated 32 and concluded that by including all developments of its competitors the MiG-23 was to be the bes

The MiG-23ML was a lighter interceptor version of the MF (Georg Mader).

basis for such a "Shturmovik jet". The MiG-23B prototype Code 321 flew for the first time on 20 August 1970 of which 24 units were built eventually. The B-variant led to the later MiG-27. Direct descendants of the MiG-23B from 1972 were first of all the MiG-23BN "Flogger-F" with simplified afterburner and laser target equipment in its pointed nose, which also had bays for reconnaissance video cameras, the MiG-23BM and MiG-23BK with altered avionics, all developed in parallel and designated

From the beginning of the 1980's older Soviet Air Force MiG-versions were updated technically in the framework of technical inspections and were then redesignated MiG-23MLD.

Hindustan Aeronautics Ltd in India manufactured 165 MiG-27L "Bahadur" under licence.

105 ■

A MiG-27M on a landing approach (Ing.Karl Brandel).

"Flogger-H". MiG-23BN and BK-variants were turned out in large numbers upon completion of testing and exported to numerous foreign buyers. The MiG-23BN for Iraq had additionally a refuelling gauge from A. D. Dassault installed. The development of a ground-attack aircraft progressed in slightly simplified form – based on the MiG-23BM – to the ground-attack MiG-27 which first flew in 1973. Series production followed in 1974 and from 1975 the FA (Aviation Front) and AV-MF (Soviet Naval Air Force) received it operationally. The same year the successor MiG-27K entered production. Both armoured ground-attack variants received the codename "Flogger-D" in the West. From 1980 the Soviet MiG-27 and MiG-27K were replaced by the improved versions MiG-27D and MiG-27M. Between 1984 and 1993, HAL India completed 165 MiG-27L's under licence given the name "Bahadur" (hero). The last version was the MiG-27KR differing outwardly from its forerunners by a changed nose. These final versions of the MiG-27 had the ASCC code "Flogger-J". To be mentioned in conclusion are the prototype 23-41, fitted with a Lyulka AL-21F-3 turbojet, and the Chinese version Shenjang F-12, which flew for the first time in 1980.

This MiG-23 is a "Warbird" photographed in the United States.

MiG-31

In 1972 OKB MiG received an order to develop a new aircraft based on the MiG-25 but with better top speed, operational ceiling, rate of climb and range. In 1974 the prototype E-155M made its maiden flight. On 15 May the following year the aircraft set a climb performance world record, and in 1977 an altitude world record at 37,650 metres. The Fédération Aeronautique Internationale recognised all these recrods, designating the aircraft E-266. Two other E-155M prototypes flew to a maximum range of 3310 kms. A further result of the tests with the three prototypes also led to the use of more aluminium in the construction of future high-performance aircraft. The first of these was prototype E-155MP, also known as the MiG-25MP, which flew for the first time on 16 September 1975. This new two-seater interceptor was to be the successor to the Tupolev Tu-128 "Fiddler" and be able to intercept Cruise missiles. Over the next few years together with new engines, the most up-to-date electronics and the newest air-to-air missiles were tried out until series production

Aircraft type:	MiG-31
Purpose:	All-weather interceptor
Crew:	Two
Engine plant:	2 Perm/Solovyev D-30F-6 turbojets, each max 15,300 kp thrust
Wingspan:	13.95 m, length 25.75 m, height 6.15 m, wing area, 56 sq.m
Weight empty:	21,825 kgs
Max take-off weight:	36 tonnes*
Top speed:	(low level) 1500 kms/hr* (over 11,000 m) 3,000 kms/hr*
Ceiling:	24,400 m
Climb performance:	152m/sec
Range:	720 kms
Armament:	Up to eight air-to-air guided missiles
(*=estimated)	

of the new machine designated MiG-31 could commence early in 1979. Problems with the fuel system delayed the start of production until the end of the year, however, but the first MiG-31's reached the operational squadrons at Air Defence Command (PVO) at the beginning of 1983. From 1986 these aircraft known to the West as "Foxhound-A" were given an extending

The MiG-31 joined the Soviet Air Force squadrons as from 1983 as the successor to the Tupolev Tu-128 "Fiddler".

The MiG-31M differed from its predecessor in the better standard of its electronics. (Georg Mader)

tank nozzle on the left side ahead of the cockpit. Out of the MiG-31M, which can engage six different targets at the same time, there appeared in 1984 eight prototypes of a more advanced version, one of which crashed on 4 April that year killing the crew. Another prototype was destroyed on 9 August 1991, but the other six "Foxhound-B's" underwent flight testing until 1992. The successor MiG-31BM had different avionics to its forerunners while other variants of the type are the MiG-31D – a

MiG-31B armed with R-37 (K-37) air-to-air guided missiles – and the MiG-31BS, a test machine for the R-37 and also the R-77 (K-77, AA-12 "Amraamski") guided missiles. The last known version is the experimental 07 which appeared in 1987, a converted MiG-31D, with RW-1 guided weapons to knock down satellites of the meanwhile defunct American "Star Wars" programme. From 1986-87 the experimental 071 and 072 were also prepared for this purpose.

One of the six MiG-31M prototypes still in existence at that time was a guest at the Berlin International Aviation Exhibition in 1992.

To the left in front of the cockpit is the MiG-31 tank nozzle fitted from 1986.

MiG 105-11

Aircraft type:	MiG 105-11
Purpose:	Research aircraft
Crew:	1
Engine plant:	1 x Kolesov RD-36-35K rocket motor, 2000 kgs thrust
Wingspan:	6.7 m, length 10.6 m, wing area, 6.6 sq.m, fuselage area 24 sq.m
Weight empty:	3,500 kgs
Max take-off weight:	4,220 kgs
Top speed:	c. 800 kms/hr
Armament:	none

In 1965 OKB MiG began work on a reusable spacecraft. One of the oldest colleagues at the design bureau, Gleb E. Lozino-Lozinski, designed the fuselage for the BOR project and also for a manned version given the name EPOS. The same year the development of a carrier system was approved, known as Spiral 50-50, for taking a space shuttle into orbit from where it could proceed to its distant destinations in space. Lozino-Lozinski took over the development bureau NPO Molniya in Moscow where work was begun on a manned Soviet space shuttle. A rocket motor was planned for both projects BOR and EPOS. While BOR would be retrieved with the help of a parachute, EPOS would land conventionally on its own chassis. In order to research the flight and landing properties at low speed it was planned to build three MiG-105 prototypes, 105-11, 105-12 and 105-13 similar in shape to the EPOS shuttle, but only the first was completed (although other unconfirmed sources say that all three MiG-105 prototypes were completed).

The MiG-105-11 was a tail-less delta-wing aircraft with a six-stage Kolesov RD-36-35K rocket motor of 2,000 kgs thrust inserted into the fuselage from above. The test aircraft was planned for flight speeds of up to Mach 0.8.

The first test flights began in September 1976. For rolling tests the 105-11 had a wheeled undercarriage and two skids at the rear. It was mentioned in an OKB MiG report that during the first tests the landing strip was extremely slippery with squashed melons. After further tests, on 27 November 1977 the 105-11 was carried by a Tupolev Tu-95K "Bear", used to test the K-20 air-to-ground missile, to a height of 5,000 metres and released. For these kinds of test the two wheels of the forward landing gear were exchanged for skids. Seven further tests followed, the last in September 1978. After that the MiG 105-11 was decommissioned and taken to the Air Force Museum at Monino where it may be admired today.

The MiG 105/11 was a test aircraft to research flight and landing characteristics of the Buran programme space shuttles.

The results of the test flights with the MiG 105-11 were an important step in the development of the Buran ("snowstorm") programme whose manned, reusable space shuttles were displayed to the public at the end of the 1980's. The MiG 105/11 was decommissioned at the end of the testing phase in September 1978 and has resided ever since in the Air Force Museum at Monino.

MiG-29

Aircraft type:	Mig-29A
Purpose:	Fighter
Crew:	1
Engine plant:	2 x Tumanski RD-33 turbojets, max 81.4 kN thrust each
Wingspan:	11.36 m, length 16.28 m, height 4.73 m, wing area, 43.50 sq.m
Weight empty:	10,900 kgs
Max take-off weight:	14,670 kgs
Top speed (11,000 m):	2,500 kms/hr
Ceiling:	18,000 m
Climb performance:	330 m/sec
Maximum range:	2,000 kms
Armament:	1 x 30mm GSh-30/1 MK, 150 rounds, up to 2 tonnes kgs payload on six pylons

Work on the project for a new "light frontline-fighter" designated 09 began in 1972. The aircraft was to operate from minor airfields close to the front, gain tactical air superiority over the battlefield against the most modern Western aircraft types, but also be able to operate in the ground attack role and as an escort fighter. The design matched the specifications without compromise and thus the MiG-29 emerged as the most modern fighting aircraft of the 1990's, whose prototype 9-01 first flew on 6 October 1977. Over the next two years two other prototypes were flight tested from which eight pre-series aircraft ensued and the completion of the first series batch began in 1982, which as

At the beginning of the 1980's ANPK MiG (Aviation-Scientific Production Complex) provided another surprise when they showed that the MiG-29 was not only the equal of the most modern aircraft in the West, but superior in many respects.

A MiG-29A demonstrating its short take-off capability at the 1992 Berlin ILA air show.

After the break-up of the Czech SSR the Slovak Air Force also received MiG-29A's.

Two MiG-29N's of the Malaysian Air Force.

For some years the Hungarian Air Force has flown MiG-29A's.

MiG-29A received the codeword "Fulcrum-A" in the West.

In the next ten years the MiG-29 was supplied not only to the Soviet Air Force and the Soviet Navy Air Force, but also to numerous export clients throughout the world. The extraordinary performance of the "Fulcrum" came as a nasty surprise to NATO for the aircraft were not only the equal of the most modern western aircraft, but exceeded them in many respects.

On 29 April 1981 the two-seater training variant MiG-29UB took off for the first time and as "Fulcrum-B" became the second most important variant of the type, for besides its training role it could carry out all military

Malaysia received the names MiG-29SE and MiG-29N "Nadgib", and from these the MiG-29SM evolved. A simplified export version for Syria was referred to incorrectly for a while by the Western press as MiG-30. Three more prototypes of the MiG-29S flew from 1984, differing from their forerunners by a more advanced inboard computer. This raised primarily their effectiveness in the ground attack role while the supplementary weight-carrying capacity was also increased. Series production of this version began in 1992. On 25 April 1986 the MiG-29M ("Fulcrum-E") took off for the first time being the representative of a lighter and more all-round second generation. At the beginning of the 1980's work began on the MiG-29KVP which led in 1983 to the MiG-

Exhibition flights by MiG-29's are always spectacular, as here in the 1995 air show at Wiener Neustadt, Austria.

purposes of the single seater. The 13th machine of the second series-production batch received more advanced electronics and a larger fuel tank, and entered service as MiG-29S alongside its predecessors. Because of the hump behind the cockpit these were nicknamed "Gorbatov" by their pilots and designated "Fulcrum-C" in the West. The export version of the MiG-29S for

29K ("Fulcrum-D") – a carrier-borne version for the Soviet Naval Air Force which was a competitor for the Suchoi Su-27K "Flanker-D". After the initial flight on 23 June 1988 flight testing began with two prototypes which made 66 take-offs from the carrier "Admiral Kuznetzov". Within the scope of further testing the MiG-29KVP made take-offs from 1987 from a ramp. After the Navy Air Force decided in favour of the Su-27K as their new carrier-borne aircraft, the two MiG-29K's were mothballed in 1993. Work on the two-seater training version MiG-29KU was of course also concluded. On 20 April 1998 the MiG-29SMT made its maiden flight. This was a version with improved electronics, great range and an air-to-air refuelling installation taken from older MiG-29's. Alongside the approximately 300 converted SMT's UB-two seaters were also modified to MiG-29UBT's. At the beginning of the 1990's an increased-value programme began in which former MiG-29's became MiG-29M's, the export version being MiG-29ME. The ME and also the carrier-version MiG-29K were known internally at the factory as MiG-33

The MiG-29M-OVT is a further step towards the MiG-35 as a technology-carrier.

The Soviet Navy Air Force required a competitor to the carrier-borne Suchoi Su-27K "Flanker", for which the MiG-29K was flight-tested in 1988 (Georg Mader).

"Super Fulcrums" and the two-seater as the MiG-33D and delivered as such to the Indian Navy. The designation MiG-33 was not recognised by the Russian Air Force. Other modifications of the MiG-29M (MiG-29M2) and K (MiG-29KUB) and the technology carrier MiG-29M-OVT led to the MiG-35 and its two-seater MiG-35D given the ASCC code "Fulcrum-F" and for the time represents the latest stage of development of this air-superiority fighter.

The Rumanian Air Force is amongst the first operators of the MiG-29.

The most modern variant of the MiG-29 at the present time is the MiG-35, whose two-seater version MiG-35D was photographed here at the MAKS 2007.

The MiG-29M2 is a modified version of the MiG-29M.

MiG-AT

In 1990 the Russian Air Force provided specifications for an advanced jet trainer as a replacement for its Aero L-29 and L-39. OKB Yakolev and MiG Mikoyan took part in the project with their Yak-130 and MiG-AT respectively. The Russian Air Force estimated that it would need up to a thousand of the successful design.

The engine and Messier-Bugatti sextant-avionics for this trainer were French and the SNECMA Lazarc 04-R20 engine was produced in Russia under licence. The wings, of compound material, came from South Korea. The MiG-AT is planned for forces of +8 g to -3 g which would enable this jet trainer to make the same flight manoeuvres as the modern types currently with the Russian Air Force, the MiG-29 "Fulcrum" and Suchoi Su-27 "Flanker". In 1992 however the Air Force decided on the Yak-130 as its advanced trainer and the MiG-AT was released for export.

Aircraft type:	MiG-AT
Purpose:	Advanced trainer
Crew:	2
Engine plant:	2 x SNECMA Lazarc 04-R-20 turbofans, 1437 kp thrust each (MiG-ATF) or 2 x turbofans (Soyuz) Llimov RD 1700, 1700 kp thrust each (MiG-ATR)
Wingspan:	10.16 m, length 12.01 m, height 4.62 m, wing area 17.67 sq.m
Weight empty:	4610 kgs
Max take-off weight:	up to 7 tonnes
Top speed:	(low level) 850 kms/hr (2500 m) 1,000 kms/hr
Service ceiling:	15,500 m
Climb performance:	28m/sec
Range:	1600 kms
Armament:	seven stations on fuselage and wings for air-to-air guided missiles, and bomb payload up to 2,000 kgs

(All performance data and the additional load are estimates

The MiG-ATS is a ground-attack version of the MiG-AT, seen here in 2007.

The jet trainer MiG-AT was developed as a competitor to the Yakolev Yak-130.

Up to 1996 two MiG-AT prototypes had been built, one with French electronics (MiG-AT), the other with Russian (MiG-ATR), the first mentioned making its maiden flight on 21 March 1996. By 2000 six further pre-series machines had been produced. According to Western sources, the Russian Air Force had meanwhile ordered ten MiG-AT, and Bulgaria two. A further interested party is the Indian Air Force. A single-seater ground-attack version of this type is the MiG-ATS (MiG-ATB) which first flew in October 1997. The ground-attack machine has the same engine and Russian avionics as the Russian trainer version.

MiG 1.42 and 1.44

In 1983 ANPK MiG made the first internal studies with a view to the design of a multi-function frontline-fighter. In 1986 as expected the Soviet Government gave contracts to MiG, Suchoi and Yakolev aircraft works for the development of a fighter aircraft of "the fifth generation" under the designation I-90 (Istrebitel 90=fighter for the Nineties), this being an opposing counterpart to the US Lockheed-Martin-Boeing F-22A "Raptor". MiG produced two different designs designated 1.41 and 1.43. After consultations with the Air Force, features of the two projects led to a

Besides the most up-to-date electronics the MiG 1.44 also has full span leading-edge slats and turbofan with thrust vector control of the engines.

The MiG 1.44 is a technology carrier for a future "fighter of the fifth generation".

consolidated version known initially as 1.42, soon after as MiG 1.44 (ASCC code "Flatpack"). In 1986 orders were placed to build two mainframes for static testing and two flying prototypes. The full span leading edges of the machine in combination with thrust vector control of the two Lyulka-Saturn AL-41F-turbofans led to the expectation of excellent manouevrability, but testing was held back repeatedly by financial bottlenecks. In the mid-1990's the development costs of the aircraft were estimated in the West at US$100 million. It was also assumed that there would be no series production of the 1.42 and 1.44, but these two prototypes would lead the way forward to a smaller and less pricey fighter.

Further MiG Projects

From the end of the 1980's ANPK MiG became occupied with a string of new aircraft projects, most of which would never go beyond the planning stage. Project 33 may serve as the best example. This was for a single-jet light fighter, similar to the General Dynamics F-16 "Fighting Falcon", to be a single-jet version of the MiG-29 fitted with a Klimov RD-33 turbojet. For a short while this project was also known as MiG-33. Designer Anatoli Bieslovet working for OKB MiG drew up plans 301 and 321 for high altitude reconnaissance aircraft. Project 7.01/701 was planned as a delta-wing interceptor capable of Mach 2.2 as a successor to the MiG-31 and MiG-31M, meeting the demands of Air Defence Command for a long-range-multipurpose interceptor. A variant, 701P, with two seats shoulder to shoulder, was thought of as a long-range supersonic aircraft but the project was abandoned in the mid-1980's. The MiG-101M and MiG-101N were the first projects of this development bureau for a conventional STOL twin-engined turboprop transport aircraft with double rudder arrangement. It followed the similar project SVB "Highlander" for 50 passengers with a rear loading ramp. After that came the passenger- and transporter-aircraft MiG-110 and MiG-110A respectively with two Klimov TV-7 turboprop engines with six-bladed propellors which could carry up to 5 tonnes of freight. An MiG-110 prototype was completed in 1995/96. The work on project 18-50, a large aircraft for business trips, was begun at OKB MiG in 1990, then passed to the Moscow firm AO Aviaprom which eventually offered its Eurasia 18-50, an 18-seater business-executive aircraft, and a fifty-seater regional airliner. Of the MiG-121 nothing is known but that it was probably a 19-seater passenger aircraft.

Another civilian project was the TA-4, a three-seater high-wing flying boat with propeller developed in concert with the Transal AKS firm which flew for the first time in 1991, but was shelved three years later. To fulfill the specifications of the Joint Primary Aircraft Training System for a jet trainer for the US Air Force and Navy, ANPK MiG joined forces with the Belgian firm Promavia S.A. in 1992 in a joint project based on the Promavia jet trainer Jet Squalus under the designation ATTA 3000. Two prototypes were built which both flew in March 1994.

In 2007 at the Moscow MAKS air fair a drone MiG-Skat ("sea-ray"), was introduced having a wingspan of 11.5 metres, range of 4,000 kms, an operational ceiling of 12 kms, drop-payload 2 tonnes. The last known new project is the MiG-LMFS (Light multi-purpose frontline aircraft), which, taking the broad view, might be designated as a single-engined MiG 1.44 although since 2011 only project studies are known publicly.

Glossary of Abbreviations

ANPK	Aviation-Scientific Production Complex
ASCC	Air Standards Coordinating Committee
AT	Advanced Trainer
AV-MF	Soviet, later Russian Navy-Air Force
FA	Tactical Aviation Front
FAI	International Aeronautical Federation
GAZ	State Aircraft Factory
GSh	23mm/30mm Gryasev/Shipunov machine-cannon
HAL	Hindustan Aeronautics Ltd (Indian manufacturer)
LII	Flight Research Institute
MG	Machine-gun
MK	Machine-cannon
NII	Scientific Research Institute
NR	Nudelman/Richter 23mm MK
NS	Nudelman/Suranov (23mm, 37mm and 45mm MK)
OKB	Experimental Design Bureau
OKO	Experimental Development Bureau
PVO	Air Defence Command
RS	Non-guided Rocket
SB	Special Bureau
ShKAS	7.62mm MG
ShVAK	20mm MK
TsAGI	Central Institute for Aero- and Hydro-dynamics
TsIAM	Central Institute for Aircraft Engine Construction
TsKB	Cental Design Bureau
UBK	12.7mm non-synchronised MG
UBS	Synchronised 12.7mm MG
VJ	Volkov/Yartsyev 23mm MK
VP	High altitude interceptor fighter
V-VS	Soviet/later Russian Air Force
VYa	Volkov/Yartsyev 23mm and 30mm MK